INTO THE FIELD
A Guide to
Locally Focused Teaching

Introduction by Ann Zwinger

NATURE LITERACY SERIES

NUMBER 3

THE ORION SOCIETY'S NATURE LITERACY SERIES offers fresh educational ideas and strategies for cultivating "nature literacy" —the ability to learn from and respond to direct experience of nature. Nature literacy is not information gathered from a series of isolated, external "facts," but a deep understanding of natural and human communities. As such, it demands a far more integrated and intimate educational approach. Nature literacy means seeing nature as a connected, inclusive whole. Furthermore, it means redefining community as an interwoven web of nature and culture, a relationship marked by mutual dependence and one enriched and sustained by love. The materials presented in this series are directed to teachers, parents, and others concerned with creating an education that nurtures informed and active stewards of the natural world.

Nature Literacy Series
ISBN 0-913098-52-3
ISBN 978-0-913098-52-3

Fourth Printing

INTO THE FIELD
A Guide to Locally Focused Teaching

TABLE OF CONTENTS

INTRODUCTION: TO LEARN FROM WOOD AND STONE

by Ann Zwinger

I believe that nature itself is the best teacher and that it's been so for a very long time. Witness St. Bernard of Clairvaux who wrote over eight centuries ago:

> Believe an expert: you will find something far greater in the woods than in books. Trees and stones will teach you that which you cannot learn from the masters.

No video, no photographs, no verbal descriptions, no lectures can provide the enchantment that a few minutes out-of-doors can: watch a spider construct a web; observe a caterpillar systematically ravaging the edge of a leaf; close your eyes, cup your hands behind your ears, and listen to aspen leaves rustle or a stream muse about its pools and eddies. Nothing can replace plucking a cluster of pine needles and rolling them in your fingers to feel how they're put together, or discovering that "sedges have edges and grasses are round." The firsthand, right-and-left-brain experience of being in the out-of-doors involves all the senses including some we've forgotten about, like smelling water a mile away. No teacher, no student, can help but sense and absorb the larger ecological rhythms at work here, and the interweaving of intricate, varied, and complex strands that characterize a rich, healthy natural world.

There are different descriptions for this kind of teaching in and about the natural world: experiential education, field work, finding the world in a grain of sand, wandering. They all add up to fostering good powers of observation and encouraging an ongoing sense of wonder—teaching students to learn from nature. All that's required of a teacher is a knowledge of some basic principles of ecology, respect and affection for the place in which you teach, and a willingness to enter a world of spined, toothed, slippery, fascinating animals, vegetables, minerals, and fungi. With their helpful pragmatic approach as well as their wonderful way with words and drawings, John Tallmadge, Clare Walker Leslie, and Tom Wessels have opened the door to teaching out in nature.

Thinking on the word teacher for a moment, I define "teacher" not only as someone engaged in classroom pursuits, but all of us who want to pass on what we've learned about the natural world to others in our midst—especially those younger than we. The encouragement and inspiration in these essays can be of inestimable help to Scout leaders, parents, doting grandparents and aunts and uncles, even some ambitious babysitters, to name a few. All can find practical ideas here for their own agendas. Passing on a copy of this book to the educators you know, as well as those who may not formally be classroom teachers but who are nevertheless actively teaching, would be a wonderful gift.

It occurs to me that mucking around in the natural world may sound great in concept but daunting in practice to those who don't know where to start. All three of these essays approach the idea of "nature as teacher" from different points of view, and suggest different ways of realizing the experience: writing about what you see, sketching what you see, and learning to read the history in the landscape that surrounds you. Tallmadge, Leslie, and Wessels each take a practical, "how-to" approach, and their essays are fortified by a deep love of the natural world as well as extensive teaching experience in it.

For those teachers who enjoy teaching out-of-doors and have been doing so for years, these essays may offer a new approach, nurture new skills, or enrich what and how they've been teaching. The variety of ideas brought together in this volume may also instigate new combinations of skills or cross-disciplinary explorations that can enhance familiar places and sug-

gest new venues for observing, studying, and storytelling about
the nature of one's community. Sometimes even the most experienced among us need reminding that there's always something
there just for the looking: the native plants persisting around
the mowed soccer field, the way water works pebbles in a nearby stream, the orderly progression of constellations spiced with
the intrusion of an extra-bright planet, a dragonfly or a
grasshopper patrolling its world with crackling wings.

If you happen to be apprehensive about teaching out-of-doors, that's easily cured by going out with someone who's already at home there; the serenity rubs off, the security appears, the confidence arrives. And for those teachers who may feel they do not have "nature" nearby,

> ✍
>
> ## Once a teacher makes the connection between the classroom world and the world outside, enormous possibilities open like a morning glory bud untwisting at dawn.

perhaps they need only to look a little more closely. There are
things to see and stories for the telling everywhere: a weed in a
sidewalk crack, moss on a wall, a busy trail of ants going from
hither to yon. Once a teacher makes the connection between
the classroom world and the world outside, enormous possibilities open like a morning glory bud untwisting at dawn, a
beautiful unfurling of inspiration and wonderment. Not the
least rewards are for teachers themselves. A teacher's primary
role may be as a purveyor of information to students, but
there's nothing that says teachers cannot enhance their own
physical, psychological, and professional well-being. The joy-
ousness of the natural world is boundless.

Trust me: as these writers assure us, there are great and good
things going on out there, it doesn't cost a penny to avail one-
self of them, and you'll have the reward of seeing changes in
students—deeper engagement with their schoolwork, their
classmates, even you. I'll never forget a student of mine who
was quite paranoid about spiders. Late one evening, practically

jumping up and down, she came to find me: "You've *got* to come see this *gorgeous* spider!" And sure enough, there, splayed out on the screen door, was a huge spider, striped stockings and all, truly a magnificent specimen.

My first true interest in the natural world came with a relationship to a particular mountain property in Colorado. Visiting one place on a regular basis and exploring it on my own, I was awash with questions: What is that red trumpet-shaped flower? What are those things on the end of willow stems that look like miniature pine cones? What owl is that whose breathy call echoes across the lake? This city girl was quickly hooked. I learned flowers and mushrooms by drawing them. I eventually learned insects by catching them, due to their reluctance to stand still for examination. I learned the animals because there aren't many at 8,000 feet in the Rockies. And with names I gained access—to field guides and scientific articles and historical records and all kinds of wonderful natural history books.

Once a teacher finds his or her own connection to a special place, discovers a commitment, delights in those satisfactions, finds the rewards of curiosity, the "ah- HAs" of discovery, the charm of a tiny grass flower or the humor of a big beetle trying to walk sedately on a tiny twig, the spiky beauty of a snowflake through a hand lens, he or she should have the pleasure and privilege of sharing that enthusiasm, that joy of discovery. A good observer can always find something to provoke comment or question, and every answer comes with a bouquet of other questions. Before you know it, you and your students know something more about the home place in which you live.

Getting to know home is the most human and necessary of occupations. To give that power of observation to students is to give them something of infinite value and importance—something to do with the rest of their lives.

Ann Zwinger *is a naturalist and author who teaches at Colorado College and serves on The Orion Society's advisory board. Her recent books include* Shaped by Wind and Water: Reflections of a Naturalist *and* Grand Canyon: Little Things in a Big Place.

WRITING AS A
WINDOW INTO NATURE
by John Tallmadge

T horeau, in a joyous moment, once exclaimed, "I had no idea that there was so much going on in Heywood's meadow!" But how did he know? It would have been easy to feel that way if he had been visiting, say, Yellowstone or Yosemite, whose exotic location and scenic grandeur would make anyone snap to attention. But Thoreau specialized in humble, near-at-hand places that his contemporaries often ignored, and his luminous works reveal the sort of wealth such places contain. As students and teachers, we can learn much from him in an era of TV, air travel, and superhighways that make the exotic accessible and the nearby seem trivial or plain. Thoreau was a self-taught naturalist and writer, accomplished from long practice, and he had learned how to use both his learning and his imagination to uncover the hidden life of places. For him writing was a form of discovery as well as expression, and like him we can learn to use writing as a window into nature, a way to help ourselves and our students discover the variety, intricacy, and wonder of our home landscapes.

The Invisible Landscape

T o most people living in urbanized North America near the end of the twentieth century, the natural world remains largely outside the range of perception. We often behave as if it were invisible. Although we may notice the presence of certain creatures or landforms, we have little idea of what's really going on. Consider the language in common use:

driving along or taking a walk in the neighborhood, we might notice "birds," "weeds," "woods," a "brushed-in" field, a "vacant" lot, or a "patch of wild flowers." Such abstractions—including the word "nature" itself—suggest a simplicity of values and knowledge in contrast to the actual variety and complexity of the landscape.

But language is only one aspect of this problem. Consider ecological relationships, which, although never directly perceptible, largely determine the character of any landscape. In the Boundary Waters Canoe Area of Minnesota, for instance, animals and plants have adapted to periodic forest fires. Jack pines have developed a cone that opens only to searing heat, insuring that the seeds will fall on open, mineral soil; aspens have learned to sprout from underground roots that can survive a swift burn; blueberries and raspberries spring up on burned areas, creating abundant food for bear and deer. The fire cycle gives the ecosystem its character, but its hundred-year period exceeds the span of a human life, and so it remains invisible to us. Likewise, in the deciduous forests of southern Ohio, trees have evolved symbiotic relationships with fungi that grow intertwined with their roots, freeing nutrients from the soil for the trees to absorb. The health of Ohio forests depends to a great extent upon this unseen relationship. As teachers of environmental values and ideas, we need to convey to our students the importance of ecological concepts and realities. Writing can help engage their imaginations with the local landscape to reveal these hidden, intangible relations.

Perception is also a matter of scale. It's easy to register things that are nearly our size or bigger: we might notice a deer crossing the backyard, but not the dozens of different beetles that also live there, nor, for that matter the smaller insects, mites, spiders, nematodes, rotifers, molds, slime molds, yeasts, algae, and bacteria that inhabit thousands of hospitable niches, from the fissures of tree bark to the interstices of the soil. The great naturalist E. O. Wilson dreamed of taking "a Magellanic voyage around the trunk of a single tree." And it's no different with the scale of time. We humans measure our day in hours, our work in days, our school year in weeks and months, our

average home residency in five-year periods. Lives and processes
untrammeled by such time frames may well escape our
notice—for instance, the sequence of migrating birds, blooming flowers, or fruiting fungi, not to mention the seventeen-
year cycle of periodic cicadas, the proverbial hundred-year
flood, or the burst of desert blossoms in a year of El Niño rain.
As teachers, we can use writing to help our students imagine
and thus entertain a more capacious and revealing sense of
ecological time.

The human past, too, leaves stories embedded in the landscape, and their faint traces suggest another unseen dimension.
Near my home in Cincinnati there is a house with a dozen
white pines in the backyard. Those trees are not native to this
area, so someone must have planted them. There is a story
behind them. Perhaps someone who lived here when the
house was young loved
the North Woods and
wanted to be reminded
of them, living in exile in
this southern land. I will
never know for sure, but
whenever I walk by, their
soft whispering, their
resiny fragrance, and the
cooler air beneath their
sweeping, oriental

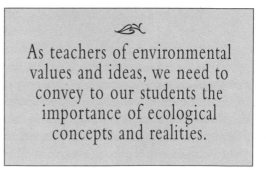

As teachers of environmental
values and ideas, we need to
convey to our students the
importance of ecological
concepts and realities.

boughs take me back unfailingly to the Boundary Waters, and I
half expect to see the glimmer of a lake. To unearth or imagine
such stories is a writer's gift—to interpret the lilac or apple
tree in the midst of Vermont woods, to recognize the odd
flowers in the triangular corner of an Iowa graveyard as a
swatch of original prairie, to read from the layered sediments
beside a Utah arroyo the sequence of Anasazi, Mormon, and
Bureau of Land Management agricultural practices.
Fortunately, this is a gift that can be passed on by teaching and
strengthened by writing practice.

Denial, too, plays a role in creating invisible landscapes.
Those of us with an active environmental conscience often

yearn for the "unspoiled nature" embodied in national parks or
official wilderness areas. We can reach such edenic places with
ease by car or plane, bathe in feelings of sublimity, purity, and
remoteness, then return detoxified and refreshed, at least for a
while, to the homely, half-ruined landscapes in which we actually live. With shrines like Yosemite glowing on our mental
horizon, it's easier to ignore the natural world at our doorstep,
which serves as a constant reminder of how deeply industrial
culture has savaged original ecosystems. Guilt fosters denial,
and denial diverts attention; we don't see, in short, because we
don't want to see, for seeing might embarrass us into action, or
at least into learning, which always takes work. But part of the
writer's and the teacher's duty is bearing witness.

Finally, we may disregard near-at-hand nature because we
have not been taught how to appreciate certain types of landscape. Glance at a list of the great national parks and you will
see that most are located in mountain or desert regions with
sweeping vistas and soaring rock formations. Generations of
artists and aestheticians, from Edmund Burke and John Ruskin
to John Muir and Ansel Adams, have taught us to value such
scenery. There is even a term for it: the natural sublime. But
what about landscapes of other kinds, those of the Great Basin,
for instance, the Chesapeake Bay, or the High Plains, not to
mention those urban landscapes that we have long regarded as
outside the realm of nature? It is hard to know what or how
to think of them. Is the strip of woods at the back of my yard
a wilderness (I found a deer track the other day), a garden
(English ivy has naturalized among the jewel weed and may-
apples), a park (it is owned by the city, abuts a soccer field, and
is designated as a bird refuge), or a waste land (there are plenty
of beer cans and broken bottles)? These woods are both
unkempt and domesticated, full of life yet all mixed up, with
native and non-native species jostling together and marks of
human activity interwoven with natural processes like seasonal
bloom, ecological succession, and decay. I don't know what to
make of them, at least not yet, but by writing about them I
hope one day to find out.

These are some of the dimensions of landscape that remain

invisible even to its inhabitants. And writing can make them visible. We have always looked to the nature writers to reveal stories in the land, but how did the stories first emerge for the writers? We think of writing as a means of expression, but it can also be used, as Thoreau knew, for exploration and discovery. An attentive writing practice can extend perception like a microscope or an ultraviolet light to reveal the unseen dimensions of our home places. And eventually, it can create stories that communicate those realities and their significance to other people.

To show how this process works, I'll discuss ways to get started: the nature and difficulty of writing, the role of imagination, the use of freewriting exercises to access the unconscious, where all writing originates, and the study of exemplary work by accomplished nature writers. Then, we will move into the field, discussing techniques of observation and note-taking along with exercises to engage the landscape and practice various writing techniques. Finally, we will return from the field to the study, discussing ways of processing the raw material of notes and memories into finished essays and stories. These three kinds of activity support the imaginative practice that will enlarge our students' vision and understanding of the natural world.

Getting Started

Writing is difficult. This fact must be recognized and dealt with before one can even think about using writing to see into nature. That is why I usually begin by engaging students in a discussion of how they feel about writing. I remind them that not only their peers, but also adults, teachers, and even professional writers tend to regard it with fear and loathing. Writing has produced more anxiety, procrastination, and despair than almost any other form of human activity. Why should this be so, when we can all speak clearly and easily enough? Aren't writing and speech both made of words? Don't they follow the same rules of grammar and syntax?

Yes, but when we speak we can use a whole array of nonverbal signs to clarify meaning, such as tone of voice, emphasis, gesture, facial expression, and pacing. We can also adjust our delivery to the response of the listener. But in writing, neither speaker nor audience are physically present. The writer must compensate for the loss of nonverbal cues by employing a richer vocabulary and syntax; as for the audience, it must be imagined, and there is no correcting a false start or dropped line. The writer often feels like a performer blinded by foot-

lights, behind which the audience sits in invisible, pitiless judgment. Performance anxiety rules, and stage fright is an occupational hazard. We feel exposed by what we write, spread out on paper for any and all to see, our weakness and awkwardness pathetically

© AUDUBON EXPEDITION INSTITUTE

revealed. How easy it is to regard the work of accomplished writers with awe: surely writing this smooth and assured must have sprung full-blown from an inspired mind. And, as if such mystifications were not enough, the culture has privileged writing as the vehicle for contracts, scripture, and laws: "Get it in writing," we hear, "It is written," and so forth. The written word has a kind of monumentality, a feeling of permanence, as if it were carved in stone; when we write something, we feel committed by it, much more so than by a mere utterance, which one can always take back or, in a pinch, deny.

All this is profoundly challenging to the ego, particularly the student ego, and generations of well-meaning English teachers have made matters worse by insisting that if we just think through what we want to say, the right words will come and the essay will flow out sounding like, oh, say, Hemingway. But it never worked like this, not even for Hemingway—though they never told us, being unused to writing themselves—and when we got our papers back, they looked as if they were bleeding. Is it any wonder that students lost heart, and still do, when asked to take up the pen?

To help students get started, I remind them that writing is a deliberate but largely unconscious act: words and ideas originate in the subconscious and are brought to the surface by noting them down. Imagination, which is the ability to manipulate reality at a distance by means of symbols, resides in the subconscious and is a survival adaptation of our species. We all have it, and it operates all the time, even when we are asleep. People who are called "creative" or "imaginative" are just more in touch with their subconscious, better listeners as it were. The subconscious works by connecting things, creating mental networks by association. This nonlinear and nonrational process is inherently playful, unpredictable, and very disturbing to the rational ego, which is painfully attuned to the performance aspects of writing. Every writer, in fact, carries in his or her head a personal editor, a sort of internalized English teacher with a wagging finger who embodies the ego's fear of embarrassment. The editor wants to save us from bad writing, which is an admirable goal, but unfortunately he or she often intervenes too soon, before the words actually get down on the page. The result is writer's block. It helps to remember, then, that the capital difficulty of writing is simply the failure to start.

Getting started means temporarily disarming or outwitting the editor, just long enough for the subconscious to begin pouring its products onto the page. (Later, when you have something to revise, the editor can be called back in.) As a first step, it helps to focus on the process of writing rather than on its end result, to visualize writing as a journey rather than as a performance, as a practice rather than as a production, as play rather than work. Peter Elbow, author of *Writing Without Teachers*, suggests thinking of writing as a way to "grow and cook a message." The master in Eugen Herrigel's *Zen and the Art of Archery* advises his pupil that if the process is followed, the target will be struck. Focusing on process rather than performance disarms the editor and allows the writer to follow the lead of the subconscious: you give up control in order to gain power, in the form of ideas and words that come welling up. Encourage students to believe that a good process will lead to good, if unpredictable, outcomes. This is called living by faith.

To help students remember the process view of writing, here are three useful maxims:

- The secret of writing is: to write. (Because you must start at all costs.)
- Don't get it right; get it written. (Because the editor should get involved later.)
- Inspiration is bunk. (Because imagination always works, all of the time.)

The best exercise I know for teaching and practicing the above is Peter Elbow's "freewriting." A freewriting is exactly that: it's short, spontaneous, easy, ungraded, and disposable. The rules are quite simple: you write for a set time (three to five minutes) on anything that comes into your head. You can't stop to think, you can't correct anything, and you must use complete sentences. If you get stuck, write about feeling stuck; anything goes, as long as you keep writing. It is best to use a disposable medium, such as a sheet of filler paper, rather than a bound notebook. Be sure that you, as the teacher, do a freewriting along with your students. As the time limit approaches, ask the students to bring their writings to a close. When everyone is finished, have them shake out their hands, which will probably be stiff. Ask them to read over their writings and underline the strongest word or phrase. Then ask them to write this at the top of another blank sheet and do another freewriting. Repeat the process a third time.

By now everyone will have produced three pages of writing in about fifteen minutes, which is a lot even for professional writers. Now ask what they experienced while doing this exercise. I have found the responses to be unfailingly rich and provocative. Students are usually surprised at the things they wrote about; many report a feeling of going deeper into the material; often they are surprised at how much was going on in their heads. Some report frustration when time was called— they were just getting warmed up—while others feel they were spinning their wheels. After everyone has contributed, invite volunteers to read. This may cause shock and discomfort at first, but reassure them that these writings are free and that no one expects great things. You, as the teacher, should also be willing to read. Four or five specimens ought to be enough. Here are two examples of freewritings, the first from a neighborhood walk, the second from a wilderness seminar:

1.) The ice has finally melted from our street, leaving runnels of dirty water and swirls of sand deposits along the way. The piles of old snow, frozen and refrozen to corny, granular heaps along the grassy edges, are encrusted with black, oily deposits of urban grime, a combination of dust and debris that's part industrial, part natural: bits of tires, gravel, soot, paper, etc. mixed with torn leaves, grass clippings, seed husks, bits of bark, insect wings, feathers, spores etc. Just as glaciers pick up all manner of soil and rock, scouring the landscape to bedrock as they plow up river beds and soil layers, so this melting concentrates all elements of the landscape. These deposits resemble glacial moraines. Thus the history of the land still lives in present behavior. I can visit the Ice Age by walking out my front door.

2.) I feel the sand on my books as I sit crosslegged on a cheat grass bench, under a great red alcove of Harris Wash. Stream clatter echoes against the soaring walls, curved like a woman's bones, so high that I cannot see the top without toppling backward. We sit in a cup of shadow, a cool goblet of darkness, writing and listening. Perhaps writing itself can be a form of listening, like prayer. Plants pray for water, listening as it percolates through sand. I listen to "meaning flowing through" the unconscious, drinking, putting forth leaves.

Now ask the students what they thought of the writings. In my experience, the pieces tend to be clear, coherent, and succinct, much better than one would expect from something dashed off in five minutes. The students will murmur in surprise and appreciation, and the readers will bask in the moment.

This exercise reveals the creativity and coherence of the
unconscious and demonstrates that students can produce a large
quantity of good writing in a short time if they trust the
process. Once learned, freewriting can be used to explore ideas
and practice composition skills.
It is a versatile, portable, and
highly effective technique that
works in the field as well as in
the classroom or study (though
it is best learned indoors).
Students should be encouraged
to freewrite every day as the
foundation of their writing
practice. They can keep a
freewriting journal using a
folder or loose-leaf notebook.

> *Study examples of nature writing, preferably based on your home region, to show what kinds of stories and wisdom writers can draw from the land.*

It is important, however, to stress that freewritings are just practice and raw material; the journal should not be regarded as a
work in its own right, and it should never be graded.

After summing up these points in a final discussion, I like to
conclude with a dramatic and empowering gesture. I ask the
students to choose the best of their three freewritings; then,
slowly and deliberately, I tear my own to pieces and challenge
them to do likewise. After all, these writings were free, and
there will always be more where they came from.

Once the students have developed a practice of freewriting,
which will give them confidence in their imaginations and
comfort with the physical act of writing, it is time to begin
preparing for excursions into the field. This involves studying
examples of nature writing, preferably based on your home
region, to show what kinds of stories and wisdom writers can
draw from the land. It also involves choosing appropriate times
and locations for outdoor work, and learning techniques of
observation that can be applied both to encounters with the
landscape and to processing the notes and memories that
result. If you are not conversant with local natural history, pick
up a field guide or two; those in the Peterson series are especially useful. Ignorance in this area can even work to a

teacher's advantage, for learning along with students always
increases rapport.

In choosing pieces of nature writing to study in class, it helps
to think of the distinctive features of your own bioregion. What
are the landforms? What sorts of trees and plants do you have?
What is your climate? What sort of ecosystems (estuary, prairie,
hardwood forest, sagebrush desert, river bottom) do you
encounter? If there are no good books or articles about your
particular place, you can choose works from other regions that
deal with similar features. Alternatively, works from the same
part of the country can be used, even if they don't deal specifi-
cally with your place. There are also a number of fine antholo-
gies, including *Being in the World,* edited by Scott Slovic and
Terrill Dixon, which is designed for writers and has multiple
cross-indexes and useful study questions. (See bibliographic section for details.) After studying a representative sample of essays
in class, you can refer to them as examples of various writing
techniques once the students begin turning their memories,
field notes, and freewritings into actual compositions.

Generally speaking, nature writing deals with transformative
encounters between humans and other beings in nature. The
mode is frequently autobiographical, and the plot often turns on
a moment of revelation
or insight. Although
nature writing focuses
on the natural world
and its creatures, it
always has some human
truth at the center, and
it always concerns the
relations between people
and the rest of creation.
Every aspect of a piece

of nature writing serves to connect the familiar human world
with the less familiar (although often close-at-hand) world of
nature, and it is this facility of connection and insight that we
are trying to cultivate in our students. Therefore, in choosing
pieces for study, look for a fine, healthy balance between fact and

meaning; avoid the merely technical as well as the sentimental or effusive. Thoreau advised his readers to "respect the fact, for it may one day flower into a truth." The best nature writing gives us the facts in bloom.

Into the Field

A lthough nature writers, like all writers, work in the study, they get their material from out in the field. Thoreau was accustomed to taking a four-hour walk each day, in any weather and often with no fixed destination. Later, he recorded his observations and reflections in a journal that eventually grew to seventeen volumes, providing the raw matter for most of his published work. Although such assiduous habits go far beyond the scope of most classes, we can imitate their structure to good effect.

Planning for excursions should take into account the teaching opportunities presented by features at particular sites, the sequence of course material, and the amount of time you can spend in the field. Excursions fall into three classes based roughly on time and distance from home. First is the neighborhood walk, which can take an hour or two and begins at the edge of the school yard. Next is the day trip to a park or preserve, which takes four to six hours and requires transportation. Finally there is the overnight trip lasting two to ten days or more and requiring the students to camp out, with backcountry travel by foot, horseback, kayak, raft, or canoe. The greater the time and distance from home, the greater the students' sense of adventure and attentiveness to landscape, which will appear more exotic and interesting. They will be more open to discovery and more attentive, at least initially, to what's around them. Conversely, distance and time complicate both logistics and lesson planning. Longer trips require sophisticated management, leadership, and outdoor skills, but the payoffs are excellent in terms of unforgettable adventures and deep engagement with nature.

The short neighborhood walk is great for introducing students to the invisible dimensions of landscape, because near-at-hand nature is most easily taken for granted, underappreciated, or simply ignored. Usually, all the preparation you need is a quick preliminary walk-through to scope out the teachable features. Sometimes, however, seeing the route for the first time along with the students is equally valuable, as you get to model observation, insight, and wonder yourself. Everything you encounter poses a question. How did these stones get here? Why are some rounded and others sharp-edged? Which are local and which came from afar? Why are these trees growing here? Can you imagine the human stories behind them? What sorts of animals might be found here and why? During what times of the year? Asking questions like these, I have covered no more than thirty feet in as many minutes; the students soon get the idea and begin taking over. Short walks can also be used to practice close observation and description, and to revisit a spot to note seasonal changes.

The day trip is still relatively simple in terms of logistics but offers a more dramatic change from classroom routine, more contact with wildness, and an opportunity to consider large-scale features of your bioregion such as geology, topography, biome, soils, migrations, ecological succession, and human history. Lessons need to be planned with variety and movement in mind, and with attention to the site's teachable features, both human and natural. The same is true to an even greater degree of overnight trips, where the main challenge for the teacher is balancing adventure with academics. Student interest runs to social life, physical activity, and food, in that order, with academics dead last. Therefore, the trip must be carefully planned to emphasize exploration, adventure, and group bonding during the first day or two, with academics increasingly worked in as the journey progresses. Water breaks, meal stops, portages, passes, stream crossings, and other natural check points provide excellent opportunities for interpretive and imaginative exercises as well as the essential practice of regular journal writing.

I have found that the best overnight trips capitalize on student leadership and responsibility. So, while I choose the route and handle logistics (permits, transportation, agenda), I give the

students responsibility for food and equipment. (Obviously, we
are talking here about high school and college courses only.)

Early in the term we hold an
organizational meeting out on
the lawn. When everyone's
settled, I ask them to split up
into groups of four; I walk
away, out of sight, then return
five minutes later and ask each
group who's in charge. This
request, which must come as a
surprise in order to work, quickly identifies the students with
outdoor experience and natural leadership. I distribute lists of
individual and group equipment as well as guidelines for
meals, explaining that each group will be responsible for planning and purchasing its own food and contributing, buying, or
borrowing the necessary gear; the leaders are expected to orga-
nize the preparations and keep track of their groups once we
get on the trail. I then attach myself to the least experienced
group as a plain member. An equipment check with the leaders two days before we leave completes the process.

I have found that this method works very well. It frees me, as
teacher, from the anxiety and burden of handling food and
equipment and allows me to concentrate on the academic side.
Students thrive on the responsibility and come up with all sorts
of creative solutions. The small groups make for more engaging
travel and facilitate social interactions and bonding, while at the
same time promoting self-discipline and increasing safety. Best
of all, no one can legitimately complain about the food!

For writing in the field, have students bring both a small
memo pad for field notes and a larger notebook for freewritings, assigned exercises, and daily journal entries. The latter can
also be used for writing in the classroom; either loose-leaf or
spiral bound is fine. The memo pad should fit in a shirt pocket.
I explain how to jot down field notes: words, images, or sentence fragments that will spark memories after they return from
the field. Set aside time each day for converting field notes into
coherent journal entries; this was Darwin's practice during his

> When writing in the field, attention always goes back and forth between the world and the page.

five years aboard the Beagle, and it works just as well for aspiring natural historians. The journals can be shared or collected but should never be graded; the field notes likewise. It helps to explain the process by which practicing nature writers convert field notes to journals and thence to finished essays and stories.

Here are two examples of field notes, one from a wilderness trip and one from an urban excursion:

FROM HARRIS WASH, ESCALANTE REGION, SOUTHERN UTAH: Sand on dry bars finer than sugar, soft & silky betw fingers, very inviting, caressing even. Boots crunch on pebbles; willows, bent downstream by spring flood, slap & whip against bare legs. Sweat dries to varnish. Pack heaves & creaks, legs pound, hips & shoulders ache. Clear & hot all day, pass close to Harris Gate where walls close to 10 ft.—how?—and just beyond the Great Alcove where last time saw white flaring trumpets of Datura Ken & Dave repairing broken pack. A white-faced Ibis in the stream wading ahead of us, curved bill, unconcerned, probing shallows, Y-shaped tracks on sand bar: peace sign....

FROM MILL CREEK, CINCINNATI: Down to dam thru brushed-in clearing. Red poison ivy, purple & white fall asters. On lake bed—drained—curling mud flats—lots of weeds—small cotton-woods, pencil thin, thick grown, thigh high. Lake silted up twice as fast as expected. Gauging tower & outflow 15 story concrete. Hi water mark— bathtub ring ~15 ft above flats where we

stand. Very shallow. Tracks of heron, deer, raccoon. Stan: 50-60 ft. of mud beneath us! You always build dam across deepest valley. All vegetation is this yr's—lake drained ~1 yr. ago....

When writing in the field, attention always goes back and forth between the world and the page. It is important not to focus too much on the page, on the writing, on getting it right, so to speak, for then the mind wanders inward, away from the landscape at hand. The memo pad's narrow format helps keep your mind on the outer world, attuned to the process of observation that is a natural historian's most important skill.

I have found it useful to think of observation as a three-stage process of description, interpretation, and speculation. This approach was originally developed by professor Bryan Wolf of Yale University, who used it to analyze paintings, but it works just as well for natural landscapes. In addition to guiding the eye and the imagination out in the field, it can facilitate the processing of notes and memories as well as the actual design of the final essay.

In the descriptive phase of observation you try to depict what is there, as accurately and objectively as you can. Show, don't tell; look, don't judge. Pure and simple. Description asks: what is it like? what are its distinctive features? what does it do? how would I recognize it? how does it look, feel, taste, smell, move, sound, change, behave, present itself? who is it? where is it? if it could talk, what would it say? In the interpretive phase you focus on relations in space and time, asking: how did it get this way? why is it here? who are its neighbors? how does it get along with them? what are its ultimate concerns? where did it come from? what was here before and what will come after? in what patterns and processes does it participate? what invisible dimensions of the place does this thing reveal? And finally, in speculation you ask: what does this thing have to teach us? how does it speak to the human world? to culture? to spirit? to the divine? what truths does it embody, suggest, or betoken? how does it address me? what can I learn from it? what is a fitting response? how should I act toward it? what mystery does it hold? why does it fascinate or repel me?

As students immerse themselves in this process, they will realize that it moves logically from concentration on a single creature or object to both a wider view and a deeper engagement of the mind, from "naked eye" to "seeing eye" to "inward eye," as it were. At the same time, ideas for all three stages can occur at any time, for the unconscious does not operate in a linear way, but in fits, starts, and startling leaps. Just note it all down and elaborate later in the journal. Things may have to be rearranged, developed, or abandoned along the road to a finished essay.

Exercises in description, interpretation, and speculation can be designed to work either in the field or in the classroom as "thought experiments" or practiced using familiar objects. Here are some examples.

EXERCISES FOR DESCRIPTION

Colors

Ask the students, "What color is a Coke can?" Red, of course, but what kind of red? Urge them to try for accuracy. Blood red? Too icky, too dark. Brick red? Too dull, too rough. Flame red? A can isn't a gas, is cool not hot, doesn't flicker or glow. It is, however, shiny and smooth. How about red as a Christmas ball? This exercise shows that describing a color accurately involves more than just hue; it includes qualities such as texture, sheen, and density. Similes help evoke these qualities by connecting the object at hand with the familiar world, and so are particularly useful in nature writing.

Now ask the students, "What color is the sky?" They'll know it must be a trick question, but most will want to say, "Blue, duh." Give them a few moments to start brainstorming. You can ask, "Yes, but what kind of blue? How blue, exactly?" Is it sea blue, chalk blue, milky blue, china blue? Is it always blue? What other colors can it be, and when? How about green, lavender, purple, orange, gray, black, or white? What does it feel like when the sky is one of these colors? And so forth. Exercises like these give students a vivid sense of particularity and help them avoid clichés, the best antidote for which is accurate observation and precise thinking.

Shifting the Frame

Once the power of simile and accuracy have been demonstrated, try moving beyond the visual. Which sense is best for knowing a given object or place? Have students try to describe without reference to appearance. Have them write a description without using adjectives, or ask them to describe how something looks using verbs. It is interesting to take different stances for observation: lie on your side, go nose to nose, sit in a tree. Or, try moving: observe from a gliding canoe, for instance, while riding in a car, or during a hike or climb. Night walks or blindfolded walks can also be very illuminating.

Simple to Complex

It is easiest to begin descriptive practice with simple, familiar, static objects: the sort of thing painters call "still life." But soon you may find it interesting to move to more complex objects such as plants, animals, or even whole landscapes. Encourage students to experiment with ways of describing behavior, change, and movement as well. Have them think about changes over time: describe something in a morning state, an afternoon state, an evening state; imagine what happens when the temperature or humidity changes; follow an object, creature, or place through the seasons.

Giving Voice to the Voiceless

This gestalt exercise works very well with groups in the field. Have students wander about till they find something that speaks to them (it may be something small enough to pick up, like a pine cone, or something big like a mountain). Then go around the circle and have them speak as if they were that thing, telling the group who they are and what they do. Here is an example from a seminar in the Wind River Mountains:

> I am a lodgepole pine growing out of a crack in a granite ledge. I flourish because no one else grows near me. My roots grope toward the center of the earth; each of my buds seeks a place in the sun. I grow, though I cannot move. My grace consists of reaching. Water and wind move me. I

weave them with light and rock to create my history. The
years have taught me how much can be gained by being
committed to one place. I do not speak, yet I hide nothing.

EXERCISES FOR INTERPRETATION

Reading the Land
The great ecologist Aldo Leopold, who taught at the University
of Wisconsin, was famous for this sort of exercise. According to
National Geographic, he would test his students by describing a
small piece of landscape—"A
road flanked on one side by a
subsiding telephone pole, then
a pink granitic boulder,
bluestem, oat stubble bearing
ragweed; on the other side a
Silphium, double-forked
sumac, another pink rock, a
fence post, and a bit of corn
stubble. A rabbit lay dead in
the road."—and then posing a series of pointed questions:
"How long ago was the last hard winter? (Two years—the
sumac's double fork.) What sex is the rabbit? (Male—females
stay close to home in spring.)"

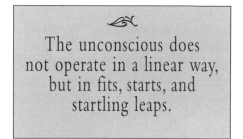

The unconscious does
not operate in a linear way,
but in fits, starts, and
startling leaps.

You can design such exercises for students at any level of
ecological literacy. It is remarkable how much students can
learn and puzzle out simply by looking closely and using their
analytic skills, once they are set on the path by a few leading
questions. The ideal site is a place that shows various relationships between ecological and topographic factors such as soil
type, slope, surface and subsurface water, climate, plant succession, and human activity. Evidence of catastrophic events such
as glaciers, volcanic eruptions, earthquake faults, floods, and
forest fires is always a plus. Students can work in teams or as
an entire class. Start from the most obvious and concrete
clues, and work toward an overall interpretation. Students are
always amazed at how much information of this kind they can
puzzle out with a minimum of natural history training. (Tom

Wessels gives examples of reading the land in the third section of *Into the Field*.)

Ecological Role Playing
Imagine yourself as a creature inhabiting this landscape; now describe your typical day. How would things appear if you were a bird? a snail? a mink? a dragonfly? a small-mouth bass? Where would you hang out? What would you eat? Who would be after you? What time of day would you be out and about? Who'd be a helper and who'd be an enemy? What would the human world look like to you? The works of Sally Carrighar (*One Day at Teton Marsh, One Day on Beetle Rock*) offer outstanding examples of this sort of exercise.

Ecological Powers of Ten
Find a place where the class can spread out; then have each person go off and find a spot that he or she feels drawn to. Ask them to visualize their spot five hours from now, then five days from now, then five months, five years, fifty years,

five hundred years, five thousand years, fifty thousand years, five hundred thousand years, five million years, fifty million years, and so on. The scenarios can be presented orally or written down, shared in small groups or with the class as a whole; they can be savored individually or synthesized into a composite interpretation.

Here are examples of ecological powers of ten from two different landscapes:

ABOVE WAUGH LAKE, JOHN MUIR WILDERNESS, HIGH SIERRA: I sit in a small flat at 9,600 feet among lodgepole pines growing in thin soil above glaciated granite bedrock.

In five months the snow will lie five to ten feet deep. In five years the trees will be a half-inch thicker, a few more dead limbs will litter the ground. In fifty years some trees will have toppled; bighorn sheep will have returned. In five hundred years fire will have come through several times, spreading charcoal; the soil islands will have spread by several inches; none of these trees will remain; perhaps there will be fewer trees due to global warming; earthquakes will have shifted some of the rocks; the elevation may have risen by ten feet or more. In five thousand years a climate change will be in progress, perhaps cooler and drier; in fifty thousand, a new glaciation; in five hundred thousand, ice will again fill this valley.

IN MCEVOY PARK, CINCINNATI. I sit at the edge of a strip of woods at 760 feet, among hickories, oaks, beeches, and box elder thirty years old. In five months it will be spring, the woods green and opaque, birds singing, flowers blooming along the ground, the soil soft and wet. In five years the trees will be 18 inches taller and an inch thicker; some will have died and others fallen; the seventeen year cicadas will have emerged, and the trees will be scarred with their egg incisions. In fifty years the silver maples will all have died and blown or been cut down; the big oaks will all be dying; the beech will be fully grown, and the hickories; there will be many perennial wildflowers on the forest floor; the glass bottles and aluminum cans I see now will be buried beneath a half-inch of soil yet still intact. In five hundred years none of the houses I see will be standing; the woods will either be much wilder or else destroyed to make way for some other human construction, but the migratory birds will still pass over head, the geese and ducks and warblers. In five thousand years the composition of the forest will have changed due to global warming; the city will have vanished or been replaced; humans may have disappeared altogether; but the plants they imported from all over the world will continue to hang on: English plantain, dandelion, Amur honeysuckle.

EXERCISES FOR SPECULATION

Speculation is the most varied and personal stage of observation, and the possibilities for exercises are correspondingly diverse. Imagine you are dedicating this place as a national park. What would you say to the people, the media, and your government colleagues? What would you say to the animals, the rocks, and the trees? Imagine yourself as a historian. What would you want future generations to know and remember about this place? What does this place mean to the human story? Imagine that you are a lawyer defending this place and its creatures from the death sentence of development. What arguments would you use? Preach a sermon on this place. If this were your native ground, what sort of person would you be? What can you learn here that you can't learn anywhere else? The richest speculation often occurs while pondering the results of field work, that is, in the evening, in odd moments of calm during travel, while resting, or especially when back home in the study working toward a finished piece of writing. Speculation grows in the soil of transformative experience recollected in tranquillity. It comes naturally and in good time, provided the mind has been aerated and fertilized with description and interpretation.

Combined Exercise: Power Spot

An excellent way to practice all three of these phases is to have students wander about the landscape until they find a spot that draws them, and then to visit that place regularly, spending a half-hour in observation and writing. This exercise works equally well in neighborhood, park, or wilderness areas, over periods of a day, a weekend, a week, or longer. Many people report fascinating results from observing over the course of a whole year. Students can share the fruits either as raw journals or in the form of essays at any degree of polish. Here is an example from a weekend workshop, illustrating how a single session can take one through all three phases of observation:

NEAR JAMESTOWN, NEW YORK: Here is a hemlock grove, open and empty as a room. Curled, yellow leaves litter the

floor. Sunlight burns through the orange maples growing
along the edge, where the creek makes a boggy pause before
sliding under the road. The flickering light beats on my
closed eyes like sundazzle flung up from a summer lake. At
ground level the afternoon light glints silvery along the
edges and surfaces of cast-off things. It's a thin, papery light,
like the kind that shines through fingernails or thin seashells.
One curled maple leaf cups a half dozen brown hemlock
needles. Everything feels warm and dry, the scent of a dying
garden in September. I feel the acquiescence of all things, a
deep contentment like the sound of cellos.

...Fall is the time that the trees give up making sugar and
wood from air, water, soil, and light. They send all their
sweetness down into their roots. In winter all life—all plant
life—goes on underground, communing with the soil. The
mind, too, seeks a return to its origins after great labors. It
craves a slower chemistry.

Amid such litter I feel no sense of waste or uncleanliness.
It's comforting to sit on the ground. Where I come from,
one can't sit on the ground without feeling unclean, "soiled"
we say because we do not live with the soil. Any unclean-
ness here I bring myself. This is a piece of land neglected by
the developers, a place going its own way. No doubt the
floor will eventually grow more ferns, bunchberry, cushion
moss, and lilies of the valley, but these things need as much
time as trees. Time and age seem to impart cleanliness—and
character—to natural systems....

From the Field to the Study:
Writing about Your Place

Whether conducted in the field, in the classroom, or in
the study, writing exercises such as the foregoing help
focus attention, sharpen perception, and engage imagination
with the natural world. You may not want to take things any
further. Some students will find short essays or descriptive
pieces challenging and rewarding enough; others may wish to

experiment with more sustained and complex narratives
involving creatures, people, and ideas. The range of possibilities
for finished work allows students to reach varying levels of
engagement and understanding. Nevertheless, it is always true
that a regular writing practice pays bigger dividends than
momentary or occasional exercises. And the discipline, concentration, and attention required to produce a finished story or
essay carry perception and understanding deeper than is possible through journal entries or freewritings alone. Therefore, we
now turn to the next stage in the writing process: completing
and sharing coherent, free-standing work.

Regardless of form, nature writing is always bound up with
place. One never observes in the abstract, but always at a certain time, with a certain intent, viewpoint, or mindset. One
never perceives things in general, but particular things, and
these things manifest themselves in place, not floating free in
some conceptual ether but grounded, embodied, rooted in a
particular space and time. But specifications are not enough;
there has to be meaning as well. A place is nothing more than
a space with a story, and the basic question in all nature writing is, "What happened here?" The place itself can be either
the setting, that is, the background for significant action such
as an encounter with animals, or an actual character, that is, a
source of and participant in the action. Sometimes the shift in
a place's role from setting to character can become the basis
for an entire story, as in Thoreau's famous account of climbing
Mt. Katahdin in *The Maine Woods*. Either way, the writer's task
is to make the place real for the reader by describing the
details that create its immediate character and telling the story
that explains why it matters.

Both students and professional nature writers begin with the
same kind of raw material—memories, field notes, and journal
entries—and both, in my experience, follow a similar path in
their creative processes. The most important aspect of any story
is the plot, the logical pattern that connects the events and
reveals their meaning. Plot makes the difference between a real
story and other collections of information or events, such as a
chronicle, a diary, or a news report. And the plot turns on a

single event, the climax, which makes sense out of everything
else. Other features of the story such as character (who?),
action (what?), setting (where?), and point of view (who's talking?) are all affected by plot, and the plot depends most on the
climax, the "moment of truth" at the logical center of the
story. Therefore, creating a story based on your own experiences and observations means identifying the climax, developing the plot, and organizing and describing events so that both
are revealed.

If this sounds like a daunting task, reassure the students that
it is also a journey of memory and imagination, a process full
of creativity and discovery. It may help to remind them that
writing is a moral act: when we write, we are seeking the
meaning in experience,
attempting though utterance
to marry experience with
values and thereby discover
coherences in the world. This
is perhaps the fundamental
gesture of human culture.
Remind them that writing is
also a means of exploration
and inquiry, a form of goalless

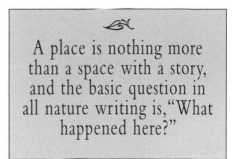

A place is nothing more
than a space with a story,
and the basic question in
all nature writing is, "What
happened here?"

travel. The great English poet W. H. Auden said, "How can I
know what I mean until I see what I say?" Each draft is a trace
of the mind's passage across the dark, creative waters of the
unconscious; successive drafts create a "map of the unconscious," achieving clarity and coherence as its wisdom and
meaning are brought to light.

It may also help to point out that the reader and the writer
always work in opposite directions at first. The reader encounters the events in a story one at a time, from beginning
through middle to end. To the reader, a story begins with an
attention-grabbing opener, proceeds through events that raise
questions and increase tension ("rising action"), reaches a pin-
nacle of clarity or truth (the climax), and moves toward a clear
and satisfying conclusion through a series of events that release
tension and resolve lingering questions ("falling action" or

denouement). This "story line" looks rather like a mountain
ridge: the basic pattern is up and down, with various false
summits, depending on the story's complexity, but always one
highest point and an eventual safe descent. (The classic essays
of John Muir, Loren Eiseley, and Annie Dillard illustrate various types of plots that engage, move, and enlighten the reader.)

To the writer, however, things look much different. All he or
she has at the start is a confusing mass of notes, memories, and
ideas, some of which may feel "stronger" than others for reasons not at all clear. This feeling of strength or significance
offers the best chance of making a start, for it suggests a potential climax and a story hidden within the welter of experience.
The writer ruminates on the material (notes and memories) to
identify the climactic events; it's a tactile, intuitive process,
more like savoring with the tongue or groping with the finger-
tips than like peering through a microscope. In nature writing,
which often deals with transformative experience, climactic
events usually involve a change in the narrator's consciousness:
a moment when the mind is arrested or surprised, a moment
of discovery, fear, or danger, a sudden insight, a brush with a
powerful animal. Its meaning may not be clear, but the event
will still feel strong and magnetic. Freewriting is a good way to
work over material and feel your way into it, probing for cli-
maxes.

With the climax in view, the writer can work backwards to
discover the logical sequence of events leading up to it. Life, of
course, does not present itself as a coherent story, but as a
stream of experiences that often seem random or disconnect-
ed. Everyday life seems more like a skein of many colored
strands than the bright, consistent thread of a well-plotted
story. If you sliced through this skein at a given moment, you
would see a mosaic of many colors, for our life consists of
many stories going on simultaneously, and the same event may
belong to more than one possible story. The writer's task is to
tease out the events that belong to the story at hand, the story
defined by the climax, and then lay these out in such a way
that the reader can follow them easily, like Theseus following
Ariadne's thread out of the Labyrinth. Again, freewriting is an

excellent way to discover significant events and explore the relations between them.

With the story line mapped out, one can begin to compose a draft. Freewritings are useful in working out ideas and angles for description, action, and exposition. Students will gain confidence if you encourage them to think of everything they do as a draft, even if it's typed and turned in; as the great French writer Paul Valéry said of poems, a piece of nature writing is never finished, it is only abandoned. Nevertheless, once a partial or complete draft has taken shape, it's time to call the editor in from the cold. There are a number of common pitfalls that beginning nature writers experience: awareness of these can guide both the composing and the editing process.

- Including events just because they happened: Not everything that happened on a particular trip is meaningful in terms of the story, though it may be important to the writer personally. Remind students that only events that advance the plot toward or away from the climax should be described. Distinguishing superfluous from necessary events is a major task of the rumination and composing process. Freewritings can help.

- Superfluous detail: Nature writing contains a lot of description, and one is always tempted to include favorite details that may not speak to the story at hand. Encourage the students to think in terms of "telling" details, that is, details that convey meaningful information and so work to advance the plot. Practice telling details by asking the students to pick out a classmate and find the one feature of their dress or appearance that tells the most about them; do

the same thing with an animal, plant, or landscape. Writing
descriptions without adjectives is good practice as well.

- Clichés in action, description, or idea: There may be nothing new under the sun, but the writer's task is to make us
  think otherwise. Since nature has been one of humanity's
  favorite subjects for writing, students' heads are already
  stuffed with received images and ideas. These have all the
  flavor of day-old french fries. Help students avoid clichés
  by identifying them in published writing (this can be lots
  of fun as a group activity; best-sellers are an excellent
  source). Remind them that, once they have been sensitized
  to clichés, the best way to avoid them in their own writing
  is to practice accuracy. Using another person's canned
  phrase is never the way to say what you really mean.

Freewriting, again, is an excellent way to practice the narrative skills that will save students from the aforementioned pitfalls. Description, interpretation, or speculation can be used as
a guide to types of freewritings. In addition, it is useful to
practice writing "dramatic encounters," a type of freewriting
that uses action and character. In this exercise you focus on a
climactic event and try to describe it as succinctly and objectively as you can, leaving out your own feelings or ideas
(except as they constitute events, e.g., a sudden revelation or
change of heart). Try to let the events speak for themselves.
Once you have written down a dramatic encounter, do a
freewriting on what you learned from it. Continue this process
two or three times to explore the material, until you have a
sense of the meaning of this climactic event, then freewrite on
what you would need to tell the reader in order to convey that
meaning. Repeat as many times as you like. These dramatic
encounters and freewritings can be shared in small groups or
discussed with the class as a whole to call attention to the
importance of concreteness, accuracy, and telling details.
    Editing, revision, and publication constitute the final stages
in the writing process, and all offer excellent opportunities to
extend the perception of nature while building community in

the class. Editing is always a collaborative venture between the writer and a real or imagined reader; hence it can be done in pairs or small groups. Sharing work in progress helps build confidence and reduces performance anxiety. And editing someone else's draft can increase the skill and objectivity you bring to bear on your own compositions.

Students can be encouraged to share finished work by reading aloud, either in small groups or to the class as a whole. A campfire-like circle can enhance intimacy and listening. Producing a class publication can be a satisfying and instructive project: an anthology of stories and essays or a natural history guide to the neighborhood can make valuable contributions to class understanding and pride. Finally, there are a number of magazines that publish student writing at various grade levels, and talented writers can be encouraged to submit their work.

★   ★   ★

Empowered by a wise practice of observation and writing such as the one described here, students can create stories that reveal the unseen mysteries and riches of their home places. Because a story is more complex than a simile, metaphor, or sentence, it can engage, convey, and illuminate many more dimensions of the natural world than philosophic or expository discourse. I like to point out that for thousands of years story has been the principal medium for the preservation and transmission of human knowledge. Therefore, when students practice natural history—that is, when they tell stories about people and nature—they are participating in one of the oldest arts. They are helping to create culture.

For most of our species' history people lived in intimate ecological relationship to their local landscapes, depending on them for food, clothing, shelter, medicine, energy, water, and all other necessities of life. They had no sense of "nature" or "wilderness" apart from the human world. Our use of such terms reveals the dismal fact of our own separation from the sustaining land. To become native once more, we must learn intimacy all over again, using such tools as our own culture

provides, and paying renewed attention to our home landscapes. Writing offers a promising path toward the intimacy we
seek, by deepening perception and understanding, by throwing
the light of attentive imagination upon the green world we
normally take for granted.

Resources and Books

WRITING PROCESS AND PRACTICE:

Dorothea Brande, *Becoming a Writer.* Los Angeles: J. P. Tarcher, 1981.

Annie Dillard, *The Writing Life.* New York: Harper, 1989.

Peter Elbow, *Writing Without Teachers.* New York: Oxford University Press, 1973.

Natalie Goldberg, *Writing Down the Bones: Freeing the Writer Within.* Boston: Shambhala Publications, 1986.

Anne Lamott, *Bird by Bird: Some Instructions on Writing and Life.* New York: Doubleday, 1994.

John A. Murray, *The Sierra Club Nature Writing Handbook.* San Francisco: Sierra Club Books, 1995.

Gabriele Rico, *Writing the Natural Way.* Los Angeles: J. P. Tarcher, 1983.

William Strunk Jr. & E. B. White, *The Elements of Style.* New York: Macmillan, 1979.

Brenda Ueland, *If You Want to Write: A Book about Art, Independence, and Spirit.* St. Paul: Graywolf Press, 1987.

William Zinsser, *On Writing Well: An Informal Guide to Writing Nonfiction.* New York: Harper, 1994.

READERS AND COMMENTARIES:

Barry Lopez, "Landscape and Narrative," in *Crossing Open Ground,* New York: Vintage, 1989.

Edward Lueders, ed., *Writing Natural History: Dialogues with Authors*, Salt Lake City, UT: University of Utah Press, 1989.

Scott Slovic & Terrill Dixon, eds., *Being in the World: An Environmental Reader for Writers*. New York: Macmillan, 1993.

Mitchell Thomashow, *Ecological Identity*. Cambridge, MA: MIT Press, 1995.

Stephen Trimble, ed., *Words from the Land*. Reno, NV: University of Nevada Press, 1995.

SOURCE BOOKS AND NATURE WRITING ANTHOLOGIES:

Lorraine Anderson, ed., *Sisters of the Earth: Women's Prose and Poetry About Nature*. New York: Vintage, 1991.

John Elder, ed., *American Nature Writers*. New York: Scribner's Reference, 1996, 2 vols.

John Elder & Hertha D. Wong, eds., *Family of Earth and Sky: Indigenous Tales of Nature from Around the World*. Boston: Beacon Press, 1994.

Robert Finch & John Elder, eds., *The Norton Book of Nature Writing*. New York: W. W. Norton, 1990.

Thomas J. Lyon, ed., *This Incomparable Land: A Book of American Nature Writing*. Boston: Houghton Mifflin, 1989.

REPRESENTATIVE WRITERS BY REGION:

Northeast: Henry Beston, John Burroughs, Rachel Carson, Robert Finch, John Hay, John McPhee, John Hanson Mitchell, Henry David Thoreau

Middle Atlantic: Annie Dillard, Thomas Jefferson, John McPhee, Donald Culross Peattie, William Warner

South: William Bartram, Wendell Berry, Marjory Stoneman Douglas, Peter Matthiessen, Mark Twain

Midwest: John James Audubon, Aldo Leopold, Scott Russell Sanders

Great Plains: Loren Eiseley, John Janovy Jr., John Madson, Peter Matthiessen, William Least Heat Moon, Theodore Roosevelt

North Woods: Sigurd Olson

Southwest: Edward Abbey, Joseph Wood Krutch, N. Scott Momaday, Gary Paul Nabhan, John Wesley Powell, Leslie Marmon Silko, Ann Zwinger

Great Basin: Mary Austin, Steve Trimble, Mark Twain, Terry Tempest Williams

Rocky Mountains: Rick Bass, Sally Carrighar, Gretel Ehrlich, William Kittredge, John McPhee, Enos Mills, John Muir, C. L. Rawlins

West Coast: Robinson Jeffers, Clarence King, Barry Lopez, John Muir, Gary Snyder, Susan Zwinger

Alaska: John Haines, John Muir, Richard Nelson

Arctic America: Barry Lopez

TEACHING
NATURE JOURNALING
AND OBSERVATION
by Clare Walker Leslie

*I have learned that what I have not drawn I have
never really seen, and that when I start drawing an
ordinary thing I realize how extraordinary it is, sheer
miracle: the branching of a tree, the structure of a dandelion's seed puff.*

—Frederick Franck
The Zen of Seeing

T he nature journal is not a new phenomenon in the history of scientific study, or, for that matter, in the history
of liberal arts education. It springs from an ancient tradition of record keeping: tribe, village, or parish records; farming ledgers; native people's accounts of the seasons and hunts;
records of scientific expeditions; travel journals; accounts of
investigations by self-taught naturalists; units of study in rural
schools. Historically, nature journals were part of the curricula
in schools throughout Europe and America, especially in the
nineteenth century and the first half of this one. In nineteenth-
century England, nature journals were immensely popular—
even Queen Victoria kept one. A classic example is Edith
Holden's *Nature Notes of an Edwardian Lady*, published in
England in 1905 and in this country in 1989.

Throughout history, scientists, explorers, naturalists, and
curious adventurers have kept some form of written, and
often also illustrated, journal of their observations, experiences, or discoveries. Leonardo da Vinci, Charles Darwin, Carl

Linnaeus, Gilbert White, J. J. Audubon, William Bartram, Thomas Jefferson, H. D. Thoreau, Merriweather Lewis and William Clark all kept journals. Before the wizardry of modern technologies, the pen, pencil, or brush was the sole way of communicating what naturalists had seen on their adventures. In our own century, Olaus Murie, Aldo Leopold, Rachel Carson, and Gerald Durrell, to name just a few, have kept up the nature journal tradition.

Why shouldn't we continue this tradition of the naturalist's journal? Why shouldn't we have the same fun these naturalists

had, poking about in bushes and streams, drawing, wondering, collecting, documenting, and sharing our journal accounts with friends? Whenever I go into a classroom, whether the subject is English, science, history, or math, I find teachers and students eager to link drawing to their studies. We have ample reason today to make nature journals integral to our own study of land. A teacher said to me recently, "Students need ways of learning how to really see and respond to what lives around them. I can now understand how the very act of drawing something makes you do that sort of aware looking."

© CLARE WALKER LESLIE

And in his foreword to *Nature Journaling*, the book Charles E. Roth and I published, Professor Edward O. Wilson noted, "The creative process is at the heart of natural history observation...it involves the illustrator directly in what he [she] observes." What is it about the nature journal that gets students so involved in watching processes, patterns, shapes, cycles, and changes in their own immediate landscapes? I still get chills watching a student, perhaps ornery or doubting at first, begin her first drawing of a leaf, then a seed pod, then the cloud shapes above, then a tree outline, and seeing her become so absorbed in the hand-eye process of getting simple shapes onto paper that when time is up I cannot get her up off the ground. The student has made her own connection with nature, and on her own terms. I have had students become so possessive of their nature journals that they put them under their pillows at night. (I always point out that a nature journal is different from a personal journal or diary. Although personal thoughts can enter in, the primary focus is the natural world around us.)

Nature journaling is hands-on learning at its best. The students are not punching key boards, responding to questions in a book, or answering questions made up by someone else. They are outdoors, looking at grasses, weeds, ants, earthworms, blue jays, sugar maples, poison ivy, and seeing for themselves connections they never noticed before. The proof of their observation is their own journal page.

In addition to offering students a one-on-one connection with their own immediate environment, the nature journal is a wonderfully flexible teaching tool. It integrates many disciplines and allows opportunities for various styles of learning. It offers students who learn visually more readily than aurally a way of using their often keen drawing skills, and can allow time not only for drawing and writing, but also for outdoor exploration and reflection. The possibilities for

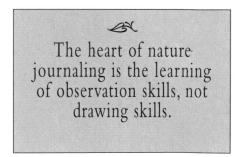

The heart of nature journaling is the learning of observation skills, not drawing skills.

individualized study are endless. Students may not only create their own journals but may mark their own plots to study, evolve their own topic of interest—bees, squirrels, local trees, seasonal changes, weather, aquatic life, and so forth.

I know few other activities that, within the space of a 45-minute class, can elicit responses like: "Boy, I did not know nature was so interesting." "I saw the day." "I forgot to sneeze." "I'd skip lunch to stay out here." Or, as one fifth grade teacher said to me while his twenty-four students were absorbed in drawing insects on shoulder-high goldenrod and asters beside the soccer field, "Why can't learning be more fun, like this?"

Nature Drawing and Nature Observation

A teacher may be thinking, "Sounds like a great idea. But how can I teach nature journaling if I can't draw?" First, let me say that you *can* draw. Everyone can. It's just a matter of overcoming the memories of the art teacher—or your big sister, or best friend—who told you that you couldn't. Anyone can learn to draw. It takes a good teacher, time, practice, and patience—as with all learned skills.

I teach a week's course in Drawing Nature at College of the Atlantic in Bar Harbor, Maine. The course attracts mostly teachers who want to integrate drawing into their classes—in social studies, math, English, environmental studies, science, outdoor education, or primary school studies. Many who attend claim they cannot draw. We draw and study the varied ecosystems of the rocky coastline, and teachers leave with drawing books filled with their studies, with ideas for carrying these methods into their classrooms, and a feeling of genuine accomplishment. They learned how to draw, in just one week!

Co-teaching with an art teacher is one option for a teacher without drawing experience who would like to introduce nature journaling to a class. But given current teaching loads, the art teacher may not have time to work with a class in science or English or history, and not every art teacher will be trained to help students do the careful, observational drawings required for a nature journal.

Luckily, it is not really necessary to draw well in order to teach nature journaling. You may draw like an eight year old because that was how old you were the last time you drew anything, but that need not deter you. If your students draw better than you do, you are giving them a great opportunity to excel in something for once. (I insist in all my classes that teachers draw and write alongside students so that they can see the difficulties students are meeting and help them later.)

The heart of nature journaling is the learning of observation skills, not drawing skills. The drawings need not be great—they may, in fact, be messy and primitive. After all, much of journal drawing is done outdoors, perhaps with the wind blowing, or in freezing cold, or a fine drizzle. Nature journal drawings are meant to provide visual evidence of what a student has seen and learned. They serve a practical purpose rather than an aesthetic one. Artists themselves usually don't consider their field sketches their best work. I once saw the field sketches of the Swedish botanist Carl Linnaeus. They were very primitive and simple, as were the field sketches of John James Audubon, but they captured the information that was needed, which is the real point of such drawings.

Even beginners soon sense the usefulness of creating a visual record of their observations. Once, I had a group of adults (most of whom had never drawn before) outdoors drawing two chipmunks playing along a rock wall. Suddenly, a least weasel shot out of a rock crevice and dragged one chipmunk by the neck scruff down inside the wall. We drew fast, noting stages of the scenario, the size and shape of the animals and where on the neck the weasel grabbed the chipmunk. We then went indoors to show the Audubon Society of New Hampshire that they had a weasel in their nearby wall. No one had seen one that close to their building. We had evidence! And I still have those drawings, marked October 24, 1987.

Though drawing ability need not stand in the way of anyone who would like to teach nature journaling, knowing a few simple exercises and procedures does help.

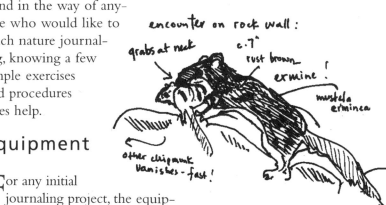

encounter on rock wall:
grabs at neck
c.7"
rust brown
ermine!
mustela erminea
other chipmunk vanishes - fast!

Equipment

For any initial journaling project, the equipment is very simple. Before investing in expensive, hardbound blank books, try using sheets of 8"-by-11" plain white copy paper and any pencils you can find. The common school pencils—#2 or "soft"—are fine. For older students, you may want pens as well—ball point or felt-tipped. Colored pencils, crayons, or watercolors can be added later, when students go over their field sketches back in the classroom.

Use a hard surface, such as cardboard, a textbook, or a clipboard on which you can lay paper and draw firmly. If drawing indoors, magnifying glasses and microscopes may be useful. Outdoors, I take along one guide to wild plants and one guide to birds for quick reference. Collecting bags are good only in areas where you know you can legally collect specimens to draw more carefully once back indoors.

I don't take a folding stool, only a small backpack with my drawing equipment and outdoor provisions: mittens, dark glasses, water bottle, several guide books, *Farmer's Almanac* for weather, sun and moon information, etc. You want to be able to move freely with your students and not be fumbling for your equipment as the sharp-shinned hawk streaks past.

I recommend having a variety of field guides and appropriate books on habitat studies available in the classroom for students to refer to. I believe that copying from field guide illustrations can be a very useful way to learn to draw. At the same time, you can show students how involved the professional artist still is today in illustrating scientific material. Have them notice the number of illustrations in their texts and charts on their walls that were done, not by a photographer or by computer graphics, but by an artist's hand.

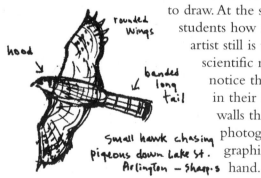

Into the Field

Before going outside, you will need to decide where you are going to go: a local wetland, prairie, desert, country dirt road, mountain trail, wooded path, park, beach, rocky coast, backyard, or schoolyard. Once there, start by observing

© CLARE WALKER LESLIE

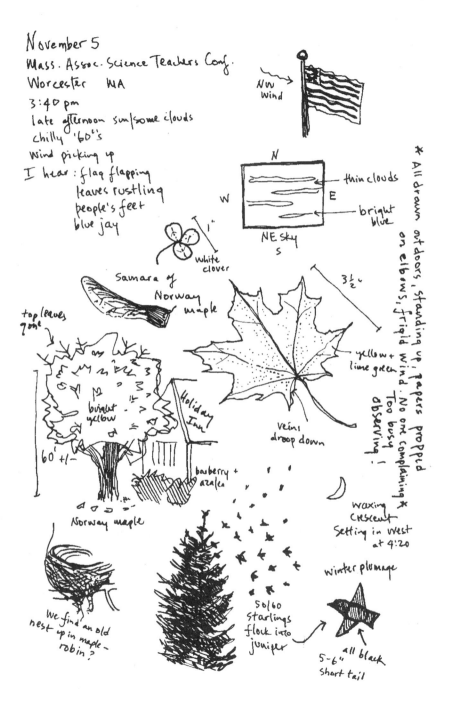

November 5
Mass. Assoc. Science Teachers Conf.
Worcester MA
3:40 pm
late afternoon sun/some clouds
chilly '60's
Wind picking up
I hear: flag flapping
leaves rustling
people's feet
blue jay

NW Wind

N
W   E
S
NE sky

thin clouds
bright blue

White clover
1"

Samara of Norway maple

3½"

yellow + lime green

top leaves gone

bright yellow

Holiday Inn

Veins droop down

60' +/-

Norway maple

barberry + azalea

waxing crescent Setting in West at 4:20

* All drawn outdoors, standing up, papers propped on elbows; frigid wind. No one complaining. Too busy observing! *

We find an old nest up in maple - robin?

50/60 Starlings flock into juniper

winter plumage

5-6" all black short tail

the season, time of day, weather, and the components of this habitat you have chosen. Decide what you want to focus on first: plants, flowers, leaves, insects, birds, or clouds.

Often, when asked to introduce nature journaling in a school, I do not know the interest level of the class, or the degree to which the teacher will be involved, or perhaps even the habitat. That's when I ask the students, "What's going on outside?" If you start in the spirit of adventure, your students will not be bored. "Is it fall, winter, spring?" "What's happening to the trees outside?" "What animals do you know live nearby?" "How would you describe your landscape?"

Let's say you are walking with the class around the schoolyard or along a nature trail. Imagine that you and your students are Sherlock Holmes, sleuthing out things to draw—varied leaf shapes, fruits and berries, animal evidence, sounds, buzzing insects, confusing warbler shadows, cloud patterns, a bird flitting by, a mountain landscape. Keep the initial assignment very specific, such as drawing three differently shaped leaves on the ground, or two contrasting insects, or two different birds on the pond. This will be easier than beginning with "Draw whatever you want."

> Imagine that you and your students are Sherlock Holmes, sleuthing out things to draw—varied leaf shapes, animal evidence, shadows, cloud patterns, a bird flitting by.

As soon as students spot what it is they are looking for, they should stop and draw a quick, one-minute-or-less sketch and label the size, color, and the name, if they know it. (Especially with younger students, it helps if the drawing has been labeled "crow," "oak leaf," "gray squirrel." That permits you to say "So, Sarah, you saw a squirrel walking a phone wire," rather than "What is that thing at the top of the page?") Students should not be afraid to have messy pages. Later on indoors, with better lighting, they can redraw something again and again if they wish, and refer to field guides or collected specimens.

Keep the first effort fun and task-oriented, like a treasure hunt, until you and your class get in the rhythm of drawing from your own discoveries. Even for students who are resistant to going outdoors, having a very hands-on and specific assignment can help. I have had students say they were "allergic" to nature or "afraid of bugs." Once drawing, once engaged looking for things to draw, the itching, sneezing, scratching usually stops.

Some Suggested Exercises

The following exercises are based on a three-hour workshop I held with ninth graders in a combined English/religion class in Environmental Topics at Northfield-Mount Hermon School in Massachusetts. The thirty-six students and their panel of four teachers had already begun writing and drawing in hardbound journals, which they would use through the fall as an integral part of their course on local land.

Before we began the exercises, we discussed briefly what a naturalist is and how naturalists have kept journals of their field observations through the centuries. We then talked about how we would describe the elements defining the land where the school was located: trees, rock walls, woods, farm fields, pumpkins, rivers, low mountains, mowed lawns, old brick buildings, leaves turning color, foxes, shifting weather, skunks, weeds, squirrels, crows, and so on. We listed these on the board under the topics of animals, plants, geology, and human features. (You can add smells and sounds too, if you wish.)

We were then ready to do the following exercises:

1. Students take out their journals. On the top of a blank paper, they put the date, and their name (if they are using single sheets rather than a notebook). I ask why date is important when studying nature. (Time of year, seasonal changes.)

2. Below the date, they write where we are. I ask why place is important to record when setting up a study. (It defines habitat and elements within habitat.)

3. They note the time of day. What effect does time have on what we see? (It affects not just light but animal activity.)

4. Then they write down the present weather, which may shift within the hour. What influence does weather have on what we are about to explore? (Again, it influences animals and plants.)

5. Temperature reading and barometric pressure can also be added.

6. We might also add the length of the day and night, according to an almanac or daily newspaper, and the phase of the moon. (In addition to connecting us with the sun and moon, this recording helps give a sense of the ancient reconnoitering of time.)

7. Next, I ask the students to go outdoors, but in silence. We walk across their schoolyard to a spot where we can all gather in a standing circle. I ask them to listen and write down three sounds, under the heading "I Hear…" These might be cars, people's feet on the grass, birds, crickets, airplanes, or whatever. I then ask them to write a brief stream-of-consciousness sentence or poem, such as, "I feel the cold wind under the dark green tree but the sun brightens me."

8. Looking at the ground: The students look down and find three contrasting leaf shapes, either of groundcover plants or fallen leaves. These might be crabgrass, plantain, clover, or a maple leaf. We use simple line drawings, and label the size and color and key features of the leaf as well as the name of the plant, if we know it. Each drawing takes no more than two minutes. I stress that these are drawings for identification, not for an art prize. We do not discuss drawing technique, even though I am drawing with them.

9. Looking at eye-level: Now I ask the students to draw three objects they see at eye-level. These might be part of a tall plant

Some Simple Tips for Journal Drawing:

1 LEAVES

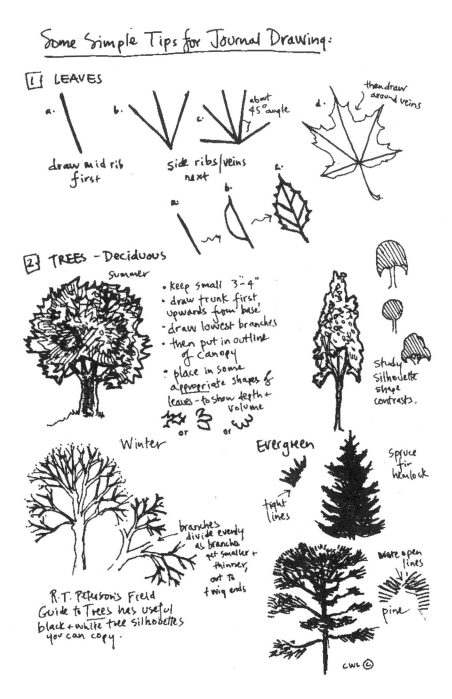

a.

draw mid rib
first

b.

c.

about
45° angle

side ribs/veins
next

a.

b.

d.

then draw
around veins

e.

2 TREES - Deciduous

Summer

• keep small 3"-4"
• draw trunk first
  upwards from base'
• draw lowest branches
• then put in outline
  of canopy
• place in some
  appropriate shapes of
  leaves - to show depth +
  volume

or   or

Study
Silhouette
shape
contrasts.

Winter

branches
divide evenly
as branches
get smaller +
thinner,
out to
twig ends

R.T. Peterson's Field
Guide to Trees has useful
black + white tree silhouettes
you can copy.

Evergreen

tight
lines

Spruce
fir
hemlock

more open
lines

pine

CWL ©

such as a goldenrod or aster or thistle; several leaves of a shrub such as multiflora rose or buckthorn; or several insects on the plant or shrub.

The students at Mount Hermon were fascinated by the various insect evidence they found on the leaves scattered across their campus lawn: several species of lady bug, mite egg galls on maple leaves, spiders, leaf hoppers, and numerous unidentifiables. I told them to draw the unidentifiables carefully enough so they would be able to find them in a field guide later. We got into a spontaneous discussion on how insects

make the transition to winter— through reproduction, death, partial freezing, and so on. Interestingly, it was the twitchier boys and the less engaged girls who became the most interested in these bugs and spent the longest time drawing them. (Here was a great opportunity to lead these students into a whole fall study on insects.)

10. Blind contours of leaves: I ask the students to sit down in a ring, and pick up one leaf to draw. They have to look at it very carefully, turning it in various positions, to try to really see it well. Then, without looking at their paper, and out looking at their paper, and without lifting their pencil once, they draw the whole outline, all the veins within, and any insect nibbles they see. The Mount Hermon students laughed, relaxed, and found they really liked these spidery drawings.

11. Drawing trees, using a blind contour: If the class has never drawn a tree before, I suggest trying to do a blind contour first. The act of doing a blind contour forces five year old and fifty-five year old alike to see a tree as the tree is, not as they think it is. I find it the fastest and best exercise to get any student drawing, no longer frozen in fear and frustration.

Using a full page in their journals, the Northfield Mount Hermon students stood in front of a magnificent, sixty-foot white pine and drew the whole thing—trunk, branches, needles, cracks in ancient bark—without looking at the paper. There were howls of laughter and whoops of pleasure as students found they had "really drawn the tree." The 36 students proudly held high their journals showing their white pine blind contours. The teachers said, "If only we had a camera." The students were astounded at how much they liked their drawings. This was only the sixth drawing of the morning's session and already they were feeling better about drawing than they had expected. They next drew a blind contour of the nearby sugar maple. Each outdoor drawing of a tree should take no more than ten minutes. (If you do not do a blind contour, I recommend the drawing be no more than 3 to 4 inches high, as bigger gets simply too full of branches and leaf detail.)

12. Looking at the sky, wind, weather: I ask the students to draw a 2-by-3-inch box anywhere on their paper. In the box, they draw in what they see overhead, and put in compass directions on each side of their box and an arrow for wind direction. During our workshop there was an apparent weather change going on. I asked the students what they thought the weather was going to become. They could see that the haze was burning off and soon we would have full and muggy sun. They were right. In New England, anyway, weather is an ever-changing and integral element of all we study outdoors.

13. The full landscape: If there is time, I have the students draw another box, this time 3-by-5 or 6-by-7 inches, and in it draw a shape map of the landscape in front of them. The steps are as follows:

• Begin with the top of the trees, or mountains, or water, as it meets the sky. Draw a line where sky and land meet.

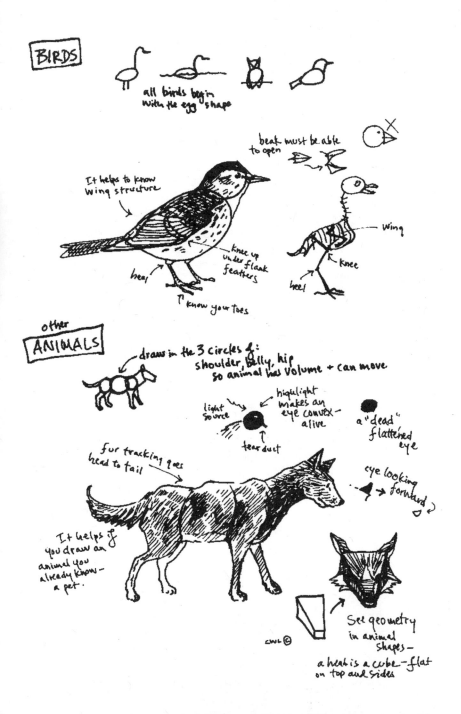

BIRDS

all birds begin with the egg shape

beak must be able to open

It helps to know wing structure

knee up under flank feathers

heel

I know your toes

wing

knee

heel

other ANIMALS

draw in the 3 circles of: shoulder, belly, hip so animal has volume + can move

light source

highlight makes an eye convex - alive

tear duct

a "dead" flattened eye

fur tracking goes head to tail

eye looking forward

It helps if you draw an animal you already know - a pet.

See geometry in animal shapes - a head is a cube - flat on top and sides

CWL©

- Drop down to the bottom of that vertical land mass and draw where trees and ground meet.

- Using simple images, draw in the trees, buildings, cars, or whatever you see within the view in front of you.

- Label what you draw and write any other topical information underneath, such as location and time of day and weather.

In this three-hour class, the students spent almost twenty minutes on their landscapes, but five to ten minutes can be fine, especially if the weather is not favorable.

14. Along the way: While a class is drawing, unexpected events may occur: rabbits hop by, a crow screeches into a tree, perhaps a hawk swoops past or even an owl. I always tell the students to stop whatever they are doing and quickly sketch what may then vanish. (I often yell out, "Draw now! Identify later.") If it does vanish, I urge them to draw it from memory. At Mount Hermon, I found one ninth grader busily drawing a gray squirrel that had scampered past, while the rest of the class was still drawing the white pine. That's what you want—curiosity and engagement.

The students at Northfield-Mount Hermon will continue with the sequence of exercises, going outdoors weekly with their class and teachers and then doing related journal exercises for homework. They will use the nature journal as fully as they can over the term, to get a sense of local place, habitat, and ecosystem.

Nature Journaling with Your Class

The exercises I have described can be modified to meet the requirements of the subject, the structure of the course, the season and weather, students' interest, and the teacher's own expertise. The nature journal can include more poetry than illustration, more plant study than animal study, more backyard study than schoolyard study. In some classes it may be possible to allow students to choose their own focus. One student may want to use the nature journal for weekly weather observations, another for careful studies of local amphibians, or a study of a local pond or other habitat through the seasons. An individualized approach can help encourage students to continue the nature journal on their own, as part of a lifelong practice of environmental observation and recording.

The nature journal can also be shared within the class or the school. Drawings from student journals, for example, can serve as illustrations for calendars and note cards that are sold for fundraisers. Some teachers have made the nature journal a group project, creating a publication for the school or the wider community.

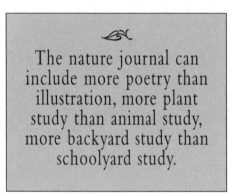

The nature journal can include more poetry than illustration, more plant study than animal study, more backyard study than schoolyard study.

Ron Cisar, a friend who teaches high school biology in Omaha, Nebraska, wanted his students to use drawing to study their local habitat but wasn't sure how to fit it into the course. The answer: Every year his honors students each choose one week, five days, during which they create a daily journal entry about their home place. All the weeks—a full year's observations—are then xeroxed and compiled in a booklet titled *A Naturalist's Journal—The Beauty of Nebraska*. One student wrote: "Saturday, April 11- the full moon is a dull yellow as it hangs low in the sky." "Sunday, April 12 - Strong winds! gusts of up to 45 mph a small butterfly fights to stay in flight against the winds." A pen drawing accompanies each entry. Ron Cisar, who has been doing this project for five years, tells me he thinks it doubles his students' awareness of where they live.

In another example, a secondary school in Delaware drew on the combined expertise of an art teacher and a biology teacher to create *A Naturalist's Notebook*. This was a year-long project in which eight students carefully identified and drew both plant and animal specimens collected from the property around the school and added their written journal entries. Both teachers worked together to give the students drawing and scientific skills. The booklet was nicely printed, in pen and ink, and distributed to the school community. Several students, I am told, are pursuing scientific illustration studies today.

I have also taught in several colleges where the nature journal becomes the basis for further individualized projects. In these month-long winter study courses, students choose a plot of ground on campus to study and record their observations in a nature journal, including drawings in pen and pencil, colored pencil and watercolor. Students write essays about their outdoor experiences and commentaries on assigned readings. The course culminates in a final project of their own choosing, which might be teaching a class in nature journaling at a local school, drawing and writing about a solo trip, creating a map of a hike, a display of drawings and specimens for a campus exhibit window, an illustrated children's story, or a detailed study of a local species.

KINDS OF NATURE JOURNALS

All of the following thematic journals have been used by teachers or students with whom I have worked:

- A garden journal.

- A drawn/written study of local birds, mammals, fish, reptiles, amphibians, etc., through the year.

- A journal of personal study plots—at home, in a park, in a meadow, on a mountain trail, at school—observed at differing times of day, of the year, and during different kinds of weather.

- Seasonal accounts: What grows in my backyard? What is there to see along my street? How do seasonal changes

Window Landscapes - if you can't go outdoors

One day I went into an 8th grade Earth Science classroom, intending to go outdoors. It was snowing hard and fast. We talked about the value of drawing/writing to document a habitat's "whole picture". Then, the students stood and drew the landscape beyond their windows. They were surprised by how much they "checked off" that they saw - just outside their classroom.

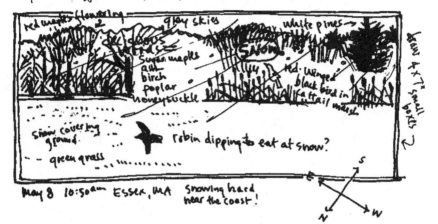

May 8 10:50am ESSEX, MA Snowing hard near the coast!

I visited a densely urban school in Philadelphia. We could not take the class outdoors. So, we all stood at the windows and drew/wrote **Nature Out the Window.**

View East towards Temple U.

affect the plants and animals where I live? Who migrates or dies or stays as the seasons change?

≈ A journal of a trip, taken alone or with others.

If a nature journal is not appropriate for your class, you might consider other ways to integrate nature drawing into your studies. A few examples to consider are:

≈ Plotting the flora, fauna, land topography, or historical changes on the school campus.

≈ A map of your town—historical, social, or geological, perhaps indicating plants and animals. Show the changes over 5, 40, 100, 200 years.

≈ A trail guide for a local nature center or school property.

≈ Illustrated classroom newsletters describing studies of local places.

Journaling and Environmental Awareness

None of the projects and suggestions mentioned requires extensive travel or exotic surroundings. Nature journaling focuses attention on wherever you happen to be, which is most likely the local schoolyard or nearby park. In recent years environmental educators at The Orion Society and elsewhere have been stressing the importance of studies that help students bond with their immediate surroundings. It is easy for children today not to notice the streets they walk on, the plants at their feet, the birds above their heads, or the phases of the moon. But this neglect spells loss, for both students and their surroundings. As the Parish Mapping Project in England put it, "Everyday places desperately need our attention—partly because they are changing so fast, and not always for the better, but also because tremendous benefit is to be gained from a personal involvement with your own locality." The link between the kind of exercises I teach and this kind of local attention was brought home to me vividly one day last March.

I was out in a small wooded lot next to a suburban elementary school journaling and drawing with a group of fourth graders. It had just snowed so we were following and drawing the tracks of an unexpected variety of animals—gray squirrels, mice, a cat, dog, crows, even a raccoon. Suddenly, over the murmuring of the children, I heard the familiar "squucking" of several courting wood frogs. The teacher knew about the significance of wood frogs as indicators of healthy vernal pools. In New England, we are working hard to protect many of these threatened watery plots. This particular bit of woods was slated to become the site of housing for the elderly. As we discussed this dilemma with the students, they grew very excited about showing their drawings of the pond and the wood frogs they had seen to their parents and then, hopefully, to the local conservation commission. Maybe, they thought, their drawings could make the town aware of what lived so precariously in the future path of the bulldozer.

I could cite many other stories about what happens when children—and adults—open their eyes to the world around them. For our book on nature journaling, Charles E. Roth and I collected a wide variety of quotations from a range of students, teachers, artists, and naturalists. This is one I particularly liked:

> Something about this January has been different from my first two winters in Williamstown and I don't think it's the weather. I think it is my eyes. January looks different...Carrying my journal with me around campus and looking closely at the shape of branches, needles, and the pattern of prints in the snow, I started to realize that life was still out there in winter, we just had to look for it differently.
>
> —Tim Stoddard
> Williams College, Williamstown, MA
> January, 1998

Bibliography and Resources

GENERAL TEXTS ON DRAWING NATURE:

Frederick Franck, *The Zen of Seeing: Seeing Drawing as Meditation.* New York: Vintage, 1973.

Jack Hamm, *How to Draw Animals.* New York: Putnam Publishing, 1982.

Cathy Johnson, *The Sierra Club Guide to Sketching in Nature.* San Francisco: Sierra Club Books, 1991.

Charles Knight, *Animal Drawing: Anatomy and Action for Artists.* New York: Dover Publications, 1959.

Clare Walker Leslie & Charles E. Roth, *Nature Journaling: Learning to Observe and Connect with the World Around You.* Pownal, VT: Storey Books, 1998.

Clare Walker Leslie, *The Art of Field Sketching.* Dubuque, IA: Kendall/Hunt Publisher, 1995.

Clare Walker Leslie, *Nature Drawing: A Tool for Learning.* Dubuque, IA: Kendall/Hunt Publisher, 1995.

ILLUSTRATED NATURALIST JOURNAL BOOKS:

Keith Brockie, *One Man's Island: A Naturalist's View.* New York: Harper & Row, 1984.

Hannah Hinchman, *A Life in Hand: Creating the Illuminated Journal.* Salt Lake City, UT: Peregrine Smith Books, 1991.

Hannah Hinchman, *A Trail Through Leaves: The Journal as a Path to Place.* New York: W. W. Norton, 1997.

Edith Holden, *The Nature Notes of an Edwardian Lady.* New York: Arcade Publishing, 1989.

Janet Marsh, *Janet Marsh's Nature Diary.* New York: William Morrow, 1979.

Virginia Wright-Frierson, *A Desert Scrapbook: Dawn to Dusk in the Sonora Desert.* New York: Simon and Schuster, 1996.

OTHER BOOKS TO LOOK FOR:

Children's Books: A number of well-known children's books use a nature journal style: those by Beatrix Potter, A. A. Milne, and Astrid Lindgren, to name a few.

Nature and Science Books: Second-hand book stores will have older nature and science books, written before the advent of photography and computer imaging, which are beautifully illustrated in pen and ink, ink wash, and pencil.

European Nature Journals: There are numerous European illustrated nature journals, most now sadly out of print. Look for books by artists such as: Donald Watson, Keith Brockie, Elaine Franks, Janet Marsh, Beatrix Potter, Rien Poortvliet, Gunnar Brusewitz, Lars Jonsson, and an aggregate of wonderful books produced by the international Artists for Nature Foundation, with gorgeous color reproductions of paintings by many of the world's top naturalist artists today.

A search by your local bookstore, library, or Amazon.com may come up with many other books under the title of Artist/Naturalists or Illustrated Nature Journals. Sadly, many of the best nature journals never make it into print. All the more reason to print your own classroom's journals and spread the word that nature journals are a superb way to integrate curricula.

OTHER SOURCES:

The magazine *Wildlife Art News* is a good resource for what is happening with nature and art in this country: 4725 Highway 7, St. Louis Park, Minnesota 55416.

The Guild of Natural Science Illustrators is an extremely useful newsletter covering workshops, lectures, and methodologies on the subject of science illustration. Courses in natural history drawing are sometimes offered by science museums, schools, and organizations: P.O. Box 652, Ben Franklin Station, Washington, DC 20044-0652.

READING THE LANDSCAPE'S HISTORY

by Tom Wessels

I have been teaching "Reading the landscape" as an approach to natural history since 1976. During that time, I have worked with people of all ages, from third graders to graduate students to environmental professionals. Regardless of age, it is a process that allows people to more deeply connect with their local landscape. It also effortlessly integrates the studies of nature, history, and self into a unified whole that serves as a useful foundation for a place-based curriculum. Only when we understand the heritage of the land, the linkages between culture and nature, and are able to interpret that heritage, does a real sense of place become possible.

Let me give an example. I live in the southeastern portion of Vermont and frequently drive through Massachusetts to visit family in Connecticut. For years as I made that drive, I missed an obvious pattern. The names of the Connecticut River towns through which I travel all share the same ending—Northfield, Greenfield, Deerfield, Hatfield, Springfield, Enfield. Why were there all these "fields" in the Connecticut River valley? Eight years ago I learned that during the seventeenth century, these towns were all established on intervales—areas cleared of forest (as much as a mile on either side of the river) by Native Americans who burned the land to increase wildlife habitat and berry production. My perception of the New England landscape has been significantly altered by my new understanding of its cultural history. Now when I drive through the valley, I can picture a precolonial Connecticut River bordered by extensive prairie, right in the heart of forested New England. This is just

one connection between culture and nature that has profoundly
enriched my sense of place.

Several books are helpful in linking cultural history to the
landscape. The one that most stands out in my mind is William
Cronon's *Changes in the Land*. It authoritatively describes how
changes in human culture induced dramatic alterations in the
New England countryside. But Cronon never explains how to
see and interpret this history that is so visibly etched in New
England's landscape. He doesn't teach people how to become
historians of their own wooded surroundings. For the interpretation of landscape history we need to turn instead to the naturalists, with Henry David Thoreau leading the way.

Thoreau is best known for his sojourn at Walden Pond and
his resulting reflective book. But few people realize that subse-
quent to this work he threw himself into a more formal study
of natural history in an attempt to know all his plant and animal neighbors. In the process he became an accomplished
ecologist. Thoreau was possibly the first natural historian to
study plants as a means to understand a landscape's history. He
was particularly interested in what his Concord, Massachusetts,
environs looked like prior to British settlement. On his walks
he would seek evidence from decaying stumps, the shapes of
trees, and the composition of a forest to infer the grandeur of a
lost wilderness. But like acorns cached by squirrels, Thoreau's
observations were scattered throughout his journals, never
coming together to create a coherent language—one people
could use to learn to read landscape histories. Natural historians would have to wait another century before a teacher
emerged to impart the language of the land.

In her 1964 book, *Reading the Landscape*, May Watts became
the first person to teach people how to read a landscape the
way we read books. She drove the point home with the title of
her chapter on bogs—"History Book with Flexible Cover."
The analogy to a history book is very appropriate, but reading
the landscape is also like reading a mystery, since it involves
sleuthing. Watts's book was an inspiration to me as a college
senior at the University of New Hampshire. It was my first
exposure to the natural history of landscapes as opposed to

individual organisms. But I didn't really learn the process of
reading the landscape until my graduate work at the University
of Colorado under the tutelage of John W. Marr.

Marr would lead us into the foothill forests west of
Boulder and have us seek clues about their history. I clearly
remember one forest where many of the larger ponderosa
pines had deep scars at the base of their trunks, all positioned
on the uphill sides of the
trees. We eventually found
evidence that the forest had
been burned, but we
remained puzzled about the
scars. Marr then took us to an
adjacent forest that had been
spared by the blaze and suggested we examine those
trees. We found thick mats of
needles, sticks, and even some
logs lying against the uphill

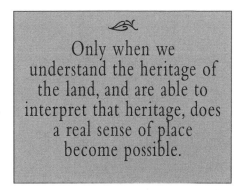

Only when we
understand the heritage of
the land, and are able to
interpret that heritage, does
a real sense of place
become possible.

sides of these trees, but the downhill sides were litter free. We
quickly realized that the trees blocked the downward migra-
tion of forest litter, creating what Marr called "fuel pockets."
The presence of the uphill basal scars in the burn became
immediately clear, and I continue to use them as the best evidence of past forest fires. Ever since those studies, my attention has been fixed on the whole forest—and the fascinating
stories it tells—rather than its individual trees.

Classroom teachers may be wondering, "But to read the
landscape, don't you have to be able to identify plants?" Not
necessarily, as we've seen in the example of the burn scars. In
the case of a forested landscape, it's not as important what the
particular species of plants are, but rather what they look like.
Are trees growing up or out? Do they have a single trunk or a
cluster of them? Are stumps present? These are the clues to
culturally induced changes in a forested landscape. Yes, plants
are the language of the landscape if you want to engage in a
close reading. But even beginners can use the kind of evidence
above to glean a synopsis of the same story.

Reading a Forested Landscape

Now let's see how the process of reading a forested landscape works. Imagine yourself walking through a northern white pine forest. The ground is level and even. The trees
are roughly the same size, a bit more than a foot in diameter,
with trunks that rise fifteen to twenty feet off the forest floor
before dividing into many, large, upward-arching branches. You
come to a tumbled down stone wall composed of rocks of all
sizes, from ones as big as a large suitcase to those as small as a

child's fist. You cross the wall and
the terrain soon slopes moderately
upward to a small ridgetop.

On this side of the wall the forest has many different species of
trees, mostly broad-leaved deciduous trees, such as ash, maple, birch,
and cherry. You notice that many
of the deciduous trees have two or
three trunks growing from one
root system. On the top of the
ridge you come upon a huge
maple that has a massive trunk of
more than four feet in diameter
and large low limbs that grow out
into the surrounding forest rather
than up, as all the smaller trees do.

The clues within these para-
graphs clearly detail the cultural history of this forested landscape. Now, let's figure it out. The stone wall separates forests
that are dissimilar in their composition, telling us that each forest has a different history—a different story to tell—with the
wall itself offering the first important clue. The wall tells us
that at one time this land was cleared of its forest, but for what
purpose? Although stone walls are often constructed in suburban landscapes to mark property boundaries, those found in
rural landscapes were constructed to keep livestock either in or
out of the open agricultural land they inscribed. Forests were

© TOM WESSELS

cleared for agriculture for one of three reasons: to grow crops, to produce hay, or to create pastures for grazing animals. The size of the rocks in the wall is the clue that helps us determine which of these activities occurred on this now-forested land.

If you have ever tended a vegetable garden in a region of the country where the ground freezes during the winter, you might be able to guess what I am aiming at. Land that is free of vegetation during the winter produces an annual crop of stones that are brought to the surface by repeated cycles of freezing and thawing. Because soil that is full of stones is hard to turn, even if the stones are no larger than a fist, farmers remove them from cultivated plots, and what better place to put them than the stone fence protecting the crops? Stone fences containing numerous small rocks are a sure sign that adjacent land was used for cultivation. Fences composed solely of larger rocks were built to keep livestock either in pastures or out of hay fields—in both cases, the vegetative cover would not have allowed small stones to surface.

Since the deciduous forest grows on a slope while the pine forest is on level terrain, it makes the most sense to assume that the land under the pines was the cultivated site. And there is further evidence suggesting that the stone wall was built to keep pastured animals from getting into the cultivated area. How can we tell that the deciduous forest was once a pasture and not a hay field or another cultivated site?

The clue is the large maple on the ridgetop. Trees with this squat, wide-branching form grew in the open, free from the competition of surrounding trees. Trees growing in close proximity to other trees put their energy into racing toward the canopy to garner their share of limited sunlight. Trees growing in the open extend outward. A tree like this

maple never would have been left in a cultivated plot, where
its roots would make turning the soil a nightmare, or in a
mowing, where its shade would reduce the growth of hay. But
it would be left to grow in a pasture to shade animals on a hot
summer's afternoon.

So we know that the forested landscape described above was
once open agricultural land with a stone wall protecting a cultivated plot from pastured live-
stock. But that is not all of the
story. The multiple-trunked
deciduous trees tell of a more
recent chapter in this land's history. The only way a tree
becomes multiple-trunked is
for the trunk to be killed while
the root system is left alive.

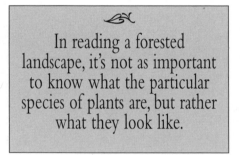

In reading a forested
landscape, it's not as important
to know what the particular
species of plants are, but rather
what they look like.

When this happens, the roots
quickly send up a number of stump sprouts, a few of which
eventually grow to tree-size. What could kill the above-ground
portion of a tree and leave its root system vital? Either cutting or
burning. There is one piece of evidence which suggests that
these deciduous trees were logged and not killed by a fire.

To interpret this evidence it may help to visualize how a
multiple-trunked tree grows. Imagine that you are looking
down on a cut stump that has numerous young sprouts growing from the outer surface of its base. As the stump decays the
sprouts grow larger and bend away from each other to avoid
competition for sunlight. In time the stump is gone and what
remains are a number of trunks arranged in a radial pattern. If
we connect the center of these trunks near ground level with
an imaginary circle, we approximate the size of the original
tree when it was cut.

To estimate the size of the original trees in this forest, we
note that each trunk is ten inches wide, with more than a
foot between trunks. Taking half of each trunk, plus the more
than one foot between trunks, we see that the original trees
were about two feet in diameter. Trees of this size are highly
sought for saw timber, but would be fairly resistant to being

heat-killed by a ground fire, making logging the more likely
explanation.

The trees in this forested landscape also allow us to create a
chronology of when the pasture and the cultivated site were
allowed to return to forest. The pines on the cultivated site
have an unusual growth form, their trunks rising fifteen to
twenty feet off the forest floor and ending in an eruption of
numerous, large, upward-arching branches. Pines, like all
conifers, normally have a single, straight trunk that reaches to
their top. When these trees were young, something must have
damaged the terminal shoots or leaders—the single, upright
branch at the tree's very top. The trunks of pines and other
conifers grow skyward through the development of this shoot.
If the terminal shoot is injured, the tier of lateral branches
directly below it takes on the role of a new leader and the single trunk is replaced by multiple branches. It is likely that these
trees' terminal shoots
were killed by the white
pine weevil, a small
insect that has a big
impact on the growth of
northeastern pines.

Weevils feed and lay
their eggs in the termi-
nal shoots of white pine.
However, not any leader
will do—the tree must
be exposed to full sun-
light and usually be less than forty feet tall. This ensures the
weevils a warm and productive haven where their larvae can
develop. The presence of weevil activity tells us that these pines
grew up in the open and not under the shade of other trees,
and since no stumps are visible, we can assume that the pines
were the first trees to colonize the site. Their size suggests that
people stopped cultivating the land thirty to forty years ago.

The trees in the former pasture speak of even earlier abandonment. Since the multiple trunks of the deciduous trees are
slightly smaller in diameter than the pines, they are probably

similar in age, suggesting the forest was logged about thirty to
forty years ago too. The logging could have preceded the sale
of the land, which might explain the abandonment of the cultivated site. We know that loggers removed trees about two feet
in diameter, which at this size were at least eighty years of age,
so the pasture was allowed to revert to forest more than a century ago. The story this landscape tells is well known in many
rural areas of the eastern United States, where farming families
have steadily declined since the middle 1800s and forests have
reclaimed the land.

Curriculum Guide to Reading the Landscape's History

As we've seen, a rather involved cultural history of this
now-forested landscape can be puzzled out from the evidence left behind. To teach students these kinds of clues and
how to use them to interpret landscape histories does not take
a great deal of time, and the sleuthing that is required will hold
their attention.

I have focused on reading forested landscapes because they
offer a wide variety of evidence to work with, are often quite
involved, and I know them well. A similar approach can be
used to read the cultural histories of other landscapes such as
grasslands and deserts that have supported agriculture or mining. In the absence of old structures like fencing, plant identification becomes more important as a way to interpret the history of these landscapes. For example, in the Sonoran Desert,
dense stands of mesquite or chain-fruit cholla are usually good
indicators that land has been grazed since cattle disperse
mesquite seeds and cholla joints, allowing these plants to pro-
liferate in desert ecosystems where they would otherwise be
less common. Those who will need to work with indicator
species should seek out local farmers, who are often familiar
with these plants and know what they signify in terms of past
land use.

What follows is an outline for a curriculum formulated
around the process of reading the landscape. It functions well

as a complete unit, but I would encourage teachers to choose, modify, and create those activities that best fit their needs. The outline is meant to be a guide that can help teachers think in new ways about how to join the studies of history and nature within their own towns and cities. All the activities suggested are appropriate for upper elementary students through undergraduates.

The curriculum outlined serves as a natural way to integrate English, history, art, and science. But more importantly it develops sophisticated skills in close observation, hypotheses testing, conducting primary research, the effective use of field journals, cooperative and collaborative work—all of which culminate in an important resource for the greater community. The curriculum has seven components that move from the study of a region's landscape history to the development of an interpretive guide to the cultural history of a particular parcel of land within the school's town or city:

1. An examination of the presettlement landscape of the region in which the school is sited and the major trends in its settlement history.

2. A tighter examination of the settlement history of the town or city.

3. An introduction to the clues needed to read the history of a regional landscape.

4. Applying the skills for reading the landscape in the field.

5. Interpreting the cultural history of a local parcel of land that is used by the public.

6. Testing the interpretation through the use of historical documents and interviews.

7. Developing an interpretive guide to the cultural history of the parcel studied.

THE PRESETTLEMENT LANDSCAPES

The central theme of this curriculum is stories—stories of
how the land has changed. I would start by having students,
without any prior research, develop their own stories about
what their regional landscape looked like when Native
Americans were its sole human inhabitants. You may want to
have them discuss their ideas in groups. You may want to have
students develop their story from a particular perspective. You
may want to have them sketch, paint, or create murals to
accompany their stories. The key is to engage their imaginations in what their regional landscape looked like hundreds of
years ago, and how native people interacted with it.

If I had been given this assignment as a sixth grader growing
up in coastal Connecticut, my story would have featured moccasined Indians silently stalking deer through vast oak forests.
This was a major theme of my imaginary play at that time. But
no matter how hard I tried, my moccasined feet could never
move through oak leaves in silence, and I often wondered how
the Indians accomplished such a feat. That question might have
led me to discover that the native tribes in coastal Connecticut
used fire to keep their woodlands free of leaf litter and the
understory of those forests open so they could quietly stalk
game and hunt with bow and arrow.

If I had uncovered this information as a twelve year old, I
would have been immediately hooked on the study of landscape history (and may have even found myself in big trouble
for attempting to burn off the understory of our surrounding
forest). Being engaged in this way, I would have eagerly wanted
to know what the land was like and how it had changed. Once
students reach this stage, they will be ready to embark on their
own historical research of their region's settlement history. If
you have local areas that approximate what the land may have
looked like—old-growth forests, remnants of prairie—a field
trip may be helpful.

Working with your local librarian, you should have little
trouble collecting books that give accounts of your region's
settlement history. Good examples for New England are

Cronon's nonfictional *Changes in the Land* and Donald Hall's fictional *Old Home Day*. Students can research works such as these and highlight findings that intrigue them, like Native American use of fire. Supplied with historical information, students can develop a new series of stories that relate to changes in their regional landscape. Their new stories should be shared in some way through readings, discussion groups, or even dramatizations.

Once the class has processed the second round of stories and developed a sense of how their regional landscape has changed, it will be time to sharpen the focus to the specific landscape history of your town or city.

THE SETTLEMENT OF YOUR TOWN OR CITY

This is the time for students to seek out primary resources. These can include the local historical society, town histories, old journals, old photographs, interviews with long-time residents, even town archives. Getting students in contact with these primary resources may involve time and travel, but the results will be meaningful.

You may want to have each student or group of students focus on different time periods or different uses of the land (logging, mining, or various forms of agriculture) and report on their findings. The class could then combine these findings to create a timeline of significant changes that have occurred in their local landscape.

After gaining an understanding of these changes, they will be ready to go out and look for the historical evidence that is etched in the land. Field trips to historic sites or buildings that directly relate to how the land was used will be beneficial. Visiting the site of an old mill that ground grain or sawed timber is a fine stepping stone to understanding the surrounding countryside. It also offers another opportunity for students to imagine and develop stories about what life was actually like for the early inhabitants of their town. What would it have been like to grow grain, separate it from the chaff, and haul it by ox-cart to a water-powered mill to have it ground into flour?

CLUES FOR READING THE LANDSCAPE

To prepare students for reading the landscape, you could review the different historical uses of your regional landscape and have students brainstorm the kinds of evidence each use might have left behind. Or you could create a photo library of the many clues that will allow them to interpret landscape histories. The photos could include a series of different kinds of stone walls and fences, a series of trees with different shapes, a series of important indicator plants, and other pertinent evidence.

Working in groups, students could develop their own explanations about why the fences are different or why the trees have different shapes, and how these might serve as clues to reading landscape histories. For example, barbed-wire fencing was first developed around 1870, but since the fleece of sheep was getting entangled in the barbs, it was replaced with large-mesh rectangular fencing in sheep pastures. Some guiding questions— would the thick fleece of sheep necessitate fencing different from the kind used for cattle?—will help students think about the evidence.

> Visiting the site of an old mill that ground grain or sawed timber is an opportunity for students to imagine what life was actually like for early inhabitants of their town.

A question I often ask my students when we first encounter barbed wire attached to trees in the forests is: "On which side of this barbed wire fence was the pasture?" After some debate, the class realizes that the fencing is strongest if the barbed wire is nailed to the pasture side of the trees so that livestock pressing against the wire push it into, and not away from, the trees that support it. By working with questions like these, students develop an analytical approach to interpreting clues that chronicle changes in the land. Later, after processing their ideas as a class, the students will be ready to apply their new knowledge to the field.

INTO THE FIELD

As you move into the field, journaling will be critical as a means for students to record what they will observe, so classroom activities on the effective use of journals will be important. I remember taking a trip with a seventh grade class before I had begun to incorporate the use of field journals. Groups of students raced through the woods, having a great time, but they only found the most obvious clues that the forest had to offer. The use of journals helps slow students down and provides the space for closer and more insightful observation.

By this point, you will need to have examined a number of sites and picked one with good evidence of past land use, and a history that is fairly clear so that students will have initial success with reading the landscape. For this first field trip in which they will test their new-found sleuthing skills, I would recommend that students work in small groups. For younger students, a parent could be asked to accompany each group. The students' task would be to seek clues of former land use, and record or sketch them in their journals.

After searching the forest for clues each group could develop their own hypotheses and stories about the forest's history. The groups could then come together and share their ideas as a class and see if they agree on a common story. If they are successful, the class would be ready to embark on their central project. Or they may need more time to develop their field skills on other sites.

INTERPRETING A PARCEL OF LAND USED BY THE PUBLIC

The parcel need not be large if it has evidence of a number of different historical uses. If it is large, you can choose to focus on a section of it. For forested areas, ten to twenty acres should do. It is the evidence at hand, not parcel size, that is most important. Ideally you want to choose a site that is representative of your region's landscape history, has some good evidence of former land use, and is utilized by the public.

My best instructional site is only one acre, but it has clear

evidence of three separate timber harvests that span a period of
130 years. During the Civil War the parcel was cloaked by a
forest of massive American chestnuts. Then around 1875 the
chestnuts were clearcut. They stump-sprouted, and around
1915 the one-foot-diameter, multiple-trunked chestnuts were
salvaged as they died from chestnut blight. The forest then
became dominated by hemlocks, some of which were logged
around 1960. The evidence of all three loggings clearly remains
for students to unravel.

   To start the project, I'd again divide the class into a number
of small groups. Initially, the groups will be engaged in a kind
of treasure hunt, each trying to find as much evidence of the
land's former history as they can. All members of a group
should have their own field journals, and a map or aerial photo
of the parcel that shows boundaries and major features. When
students discover any evidence of past land use, or even a feature that is puzzling, they should mark its approximate position
on the map and then sketch the evidence in their journal,
adding pertinent comments to further detail what they
observe. Journals will be the students' sole record of what they
find. They will repeatedly refer to them back in class, and use
them for the development of the interpretive guide.

   After the modified treasure hunt, each group could tran-
scribe what they found onto a large map back in the classroom. This map would be used by all the groups to construct
their interpretation of the parcel's history. Their task should be
to decide how many different human activities occurred on
the land and then develop a chronology of these uses. Each
group would then present their chronological story to the class
for consideration and discussion.

   After all groups have reported, there will likely be agree-
ment on certain aspects of the land's history and disagreement
on others. For example, there is evidence of a fire in my
favorite instructional site, and students often debate about
whether the fire came before or after the salvaging of the multiple-trunked chestnuts. Disagreements may serve as the focus
for further field investigations, to look for evidence to further
support or reject the contested interpretations. When agree-

ment is reached on the parcel's history, the class will be ready
to test their interpretation.

TESTING THE CLASS INTERPRETATION

To test their landscape history, students will again need to refer
to historical documents, including town histories, old journals,
old photographs, past aerial photos, deed searches, and interviews with long-time residents. Each group could be assigned
one avenue to investigate, either interviews, deed searches, or
old photographs, and then present their findings to the whole
class. It will be the combination of these findings and their
own field-based sleuthing that will frame the story of the parcel's history and the development of the interpretive guide.

DEVELOPING THE INTERPRETIVE GUIDE

Because there are many approaches to producing an interpretive guide, I won't try to prescribe any one in particular, but I
do have a few recommendations.

Working in groups, students should be responsible for
developing proposals regarding the form and content of the
guide. These can be shared with the class, and once a consen-
sus is reached, the teacher should then oversee the guide's
development. This may involve creating new work groups to
write text, transpose journal sketches that clearly display
important evidence, create the general design of the guide,
and develop its layout.

The guide could take any number of forms—a booklet to
be carried while walking the trail, or a kiosk at the start of the
trail that points out highlights of the parcel's cultural history. It
may be signage along the trail (however, signs are prone to
vandalism and require more maintenance). It could point out
evidence of former land use adjacent to an already established
trail, or a trail system may be developed that leads visitors to
pertinent sites. (The class need not create the trail if other
groups, clubs, or organizations in the school or town become
interested in the project.)

Whatever form the guide takes, it should tell a good story, be illustrated with sketches from the students' journals, and should pose questions that will make the visitor ponder the evidence. Rather than simply pointing out—"the squat, wide-branching tree was left to shade pastured livestock." The guide might ask, "Why is the shape of this large tree so different? What does it tells us about the past history of the land?" The answer can then be teased out. The guide is meant to open the eyes of local citizens to the dynamic history of their landscape, and peoples' eyes are opened more by questions than answers.

A class may wish to introduce the guide to the public through some form of opening ceremony. Students will have worked hard to get this far and they should be recognized for their efforts. Using local media, they could advertise the opening as an important community event. Students could take an active role in leading workshops on the region's cultural history, the process of producing the interpretive guide, or they might want to lead interpretive walks. However it is conducted, an opening ceremony would be important. It forms the critical link between the students, the community, and their cultural heritage. It should be a time for shared celebration.

Making It Happen

To implement all the suggested activities will take a good amount of classroom time. For middle and secondary schools, it may be necessary to integrate several courses to create blocks of time for field investigations. Just one classroom day a week or every other week could be dedicated to the above activities, so required content in each of the disciplines could still be covered. I found this to be a very successful model for scheduling when I worked at the Putney School in Vermont, where I was part of a teaching team that developed an integrated curriculum for juniors involving courses in ecology, American history, and American literature. Each course had ample time to cover required content, and yet we still had large blocks of time to effectively integrate the three courses.

Some teachers will wish to choose from the above activities, or add their own. For those who want to focus on the interpretive guide but can't commit to all the listed activities, I'd suggest dropping the first two. Any teacher wanting to tackle all the suggested activities will need to invest a good amount of preparation time (I'd suggest that planning start a year in advance). However, you need not do this all on your own. Every town or city will have ample resources to help you. At the very start contact your local historical society, town historian, or your local librarian. Enlist their help to gather books and primary documents about the region's

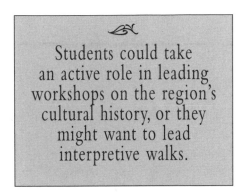

Students could take an active role in leading workshops on the region's cultural history, or they might want to lead interpretive walks.

and town's settlement history. If your town or city has a historical society ask for volunteers to help students conduct research. Getting residents on board will greatly reduce your own investment of time.

Next seek out your local naturalists. Try contacting a local chapter of the Audubon Society or similar organization, a nature center, a resident forester, biologists from a state university's extension service, or a regional conservation organization. All can help you quickly develop skills in reading the landscape and point you to pertinent resources and sites. They may even be enlisted as volunteers to help with field trips or scoping potential field sites. Be sure to contact the Natural Resources Conservation Service (formerly the Soil Conservation Service) to get aerial photos of your area, both old and recent. These resources will make your task easier and far richer.

If you need funds to help defray costs of field trips or to produce your interpretive guide, once again, don't be shy about asking for assistance. Garden clubs, historical societies, civic groups like the Lions or Kiwanas Club, not to mention local businesses, all fund local projects like this one. You may be surprised just how much monetary support you will be able to muster for a well-articulated, community-based project.

You will also need to begin your own research. Again your local librarian and naturalists will be most helpful here in suggesting books on your region's settlement and natural history. The following book list contains the best resources with which I am familiar for linking culture to changes in the land. All are geared to regions east of the Mississippi, but, when linked with books of more regional focus, will still be helpful to anyone wanting to learn the process of reading the landscape. For regional natural history, I also find the Sierra Club Naturalist Guides to be quite good. Following the book list is an appendix from my book, *Reading the Forested Landscape*, on evidence that can be used to read forested landscapes in the Northeast.

Although developing a unit on reading cultural changes in the landscape demands an investment of your time and energy, I can assure you it will be well spent. The result will be a dynamic, integrated study that not only develops a wide array of skills, but links students and community members in meaningful ways to the stories told by their local landscapes.

Reference Books:

Susan Allport, *Sermons in Stone: The Stone Walls of New England and New York*. New York: W. W. Norton & Company, 1990.
An excellent account of the Northeast's rural landscape during the 18th and 19th centuries through an examination of stone walls. Richly illustrated.

William Cronon, *Changes in the Land: Indians, Colonists, and the Ecology of New England*. New York: Hill and Wang, 1983.
The most authoritative book on the relationship between human culture and changing landscapes. Thoroughly researched.

Gordon Whitney, *From Coastal Wilderness to Fruited Plain: A History of Environmental Change in Temperate North America 1500-Present*. Cambridge: Cambridge University Press, 1994.
The most comprehensive review of the changing landscape of the eastern United States. The introductory photo essay of the region's original forest types is striking.

Donald Hall, *Old Home Day*. New York: Harcourt Brace & Company, 1996.
An accurate children's book that follows the changes in the landscape of a New England town from the last ice age to its 1999 bicentennial.

Gary Paulsen, *The Island*. New York: Bantam Doubleday Dell, 1988.
The journal of a fourteen-year-old boy who moves from Madison to the northern wilds of Wisconsin. It serves as a wonderful model for linking close observation with journaling.

Bonnie Pryor, *The House on Maple Street*. New York: Mulberry Books, 1987.
A children's book that traces changes in the land from pre-settlement to a modern suburban community.

Betty Flanders Thompson, *The Changing Face of New England.*
New York: Macmillan, 1958.
The first book to outline the grand changes that have taken
place in New England's landscape.

May T. Watts, *Reading the Landscape in America.* Rochester, NY:
Nature Study Guild Publishers, 1999, 3rd ed.
The ground-breaking book that explains how to read land-
scape histories throughout the United States.

Tom Wessels, *Reading the Forested Landscape: A Natural History
of New England.* Woodstock, VT: The Countryman Press. 1997.
A detailed account of how to read forest histories. Richly
illustrated.

Evidence of Former Disturbance in Forested Landscapes

FIRE

⚘ *Standing Dead Snags*
Conifers and oaks that are made rot-resistant by heat stand
for many decades and are often silvery in appearance and free
of fungi.

⚘ *Discontinuity in Age Classes*
Fires often leave the overstory intact and create a vigorous
understory, but usually remove the mid-story trees. Logging
will not do this; an age discontinuity can only be observed in
forests with trees more than two feet in diameter.

⚘ *Basal Fire Scar*
On a slope, triangular basal scars appear on the uphill sides of
trees where fuel pockets formed. If trees are not on a slope, the
scars will be randomly distributed.

⚘ *Multiple-Trunked Trees*
Many broad-leaved trees and some pines send up stump sprouts
after their trunks have been heat killed.

ଛ Charcoal

After ten years charcoal is not very visible unless one digs in the soil, and even then it may not be found. Since certain fungi that grow on decaying sugar maple and beech look very much like charcoal, fire should always be verified by means other than just charcoal alone.

PASTURING

ଛ Stonewalls

Constructed only with large stones, the presence of many fist-sized stones indicates past cultivation.

ଛ Barbed Wire

Barbed wire was first used in the early 1870s. Its presence indicates pastures that were used in the last century.

ଛ Pasture Trees

Wide, low-branching trees were left to shade livestock when woods were cleared. Thorny shrubs—hawthorns, barberry, and roses—all deter browsing.

ଛ Juniper

This slow-growing, unpalatable shrub thrives on grazed land where grass would otherwise overtop and kill it. The only other sites in which it is commonly found are on rock outcrops and on poor coarse soils where herbaceous vegetation is lacking.

ଛ Weird Apples

Apple trees that are highly contorted at the base and have many dead basal branches near the ground are a result of heavy browsing.

LOGGING

ଛ Multiple-Trunked Trees

Many broad-leaved trees send up stump sprouts after they have been cut.

🌢 *Cut Stumps*
These stumps have a visible flat top.

🌢 *Opposing Basal Scars*
The skidding of logs damages the bases of trees on skidder roads, creating basal scars that face one another across the road and are often triangular in shape.

🌢 *Softwood Stumps*
Softwood stumps decay from the outside in.

🌢 *Rot-Resistant Hardwood Stumps*
These stumps decay from the inside out.

BLIGHTS
🌢 *Snags with Fungus*
Trees killed by blights (insect or fungal) are not rot-resistant and quickly develop fungi. The exceptions are American chestnut, and oaks—both are naturally rot-resistant.

BEAVER ACTIVITY
🌢 *Standing Dead Snags in Water*
Flooding kills trees, but the anaerobic conditions created by the flooding preserves the root systems, allowing dead snags to remain standing for decades. These trees are usually conifers and birches.

🌢 *Beaver Cut Stumps*
Blond-colored stumps indicate beaver activity within the year, gray stumps were cut more than a year ago, and stumps with turkey-tail fungi growing on them were cut at least three years ago.

🌢 *Beaver Dams*
The first sign of beaver abandonment is a drop in water level below the top of the dam. Herbaceous vegetation growing on the pond side of the dam indicates abandonment of at least two months. Woody vegetation growing on the pond side

indicates abandonment of at least two years.

BLOW DOWNS
ℬ *Downed Trees*
Trees all lying in the same direction indicate that they were blown down. Downed trees lying in all directions indicate that dead trees fell over at various times.

ℬ *Pillow and Cradle Topography*
When a live tree is blown over, its upended roots carry a lot of earth, creating a depression or "cradle" where it grew. When the tree and root system rot, the earth is dropped as a pile or "pillow" next to the cradle. Pillow and cradle topography lasts for hundreds of years.

ℬ *Nurse Logs*
Most often hemlock trees growing in a line with exposed roots tracing the line indicate a former nurse log—a decaying log on which trees grow.

Author Biographies

CLARE WALKER LESLIE is a nationally recognized wildlife artist, naturalist, educator, and author of five books, including *Nature Journaling: Learning to Observe and Connect with the World Around You*, co-authored with Charles E. Roth, *The Art of Field Sketching*, *Nature Drawing: A Tool for Learning*, and the children's book *Nature All Year Long*. She has been teaching nature journaling and field sketching for over twenty-five years in grade schools, colleges, art schools, nature centers, conferences, and adult education programs. With a B.A. in art history and experience studying wildlife drawing and watercolor techniques in England, Scotland, and Sweden, Clare brings an attentive eye to teaching the use of the field journal and skills for observing the natural world throughout the year. Clare and her family split their time between Granville, Vermont, and Cambridge, Massachusetts.

JOHN TALLMADGE is core professor in literature and environmental studies at the Graduate College of the Union Institute, where he also served as associate and acting dean. Educated at Dartmouth College (B.A.) and Yale University (Ph.D.), he has held regular teaching positions at the University of Utah and Carleton College and has acted as a consultant for various colleges, universities, and private institutions concerned with environmental education. His writings include *Meeting the Tree of Life*, a memoir of teaching and wilderness travel, as well as numerous critical and personal essays on wilderness, environmental philosophy, and nature writing, and book reviews in *Orion* and *The New York Times Book Review* as well as various learned journals. He currently lives with his wife and daughters in Cincinnati, Ohio, and is at work on a book about learning from nature in the city.

As a terrestrial ecologist interested in alpine, desert, and forest
ecosystems, **TOM WESSELS** considers himself a generalist with
an avocation for teaching and writing. With over twenty years
of experience as an educator, Tom has taught at the secondary,
undergraduate, and graduate levels. He is presently director of
the Environmental Biology Program at Antioch New England
Graduate School in Keene, New Hampshire. His inquiry-based
teaching style is strongly incorporated into his book, *Reading
the Forested Landscape: A Natural History of New England*. His
interest in forest management strategies that promote diversity
at the landscape level has led him to consult for the Rain
Forest Alliance's Smart Wood program, helping to develop
"green certification" guidelines for the northeastern United
States. When not teaching, consulting, writing, or attempting
to finish the house he started in 1978, Tom can be found ram-
bling through the fields and forests of southeastern Vermont.

The ORION Society

The Orion Society's mission is to inform, inspire, and engage individuals and grassroots organizations across North America in becoming a significant cultural force for healing nature and community.

Our programs and publications include:

Orion Magazine

In both print and online editions, *Orion* is an award-winning, advertising-free bimonthly pushing at the frontiers of nature stewardship and social responsibility. The magazine serves as a source of provocative, fresh thinking for educators, activists, and concerned citizens.

Orion Grassroots Network

OGN connects the full diversity of nonprofits engaged in the social and environmental movements of North America and beyond and offers them training, a job and internship bulletin board, and other services to help them operate most effectively.

Orion Education

As an alternative to narrowly conceived schooling with heavy reliance on tests, Orion advocates for Whole Child Education. This approach gets children outside the classroom for programs and projects that require them to use multiple disciplines and develop initiative, imagination, teamwork, and other skills. *Into the Field*, as developed in Orion's Nature Literacy Series books, is one application of this approach.

The Orion Society is a 501(c)3 organization. Our programs and publications are made possible in part due to generous donations from individuals, corporations, and foundations. Learn more at www.orionsociety.org.